Music Production Mastery:

All You Need to Know About Producing Music, Songwriting, Music Theory and Creativity (Two Book Bundle)

Copyright Notice

Disclaimer

Claim This Now

In the Mix Discover the Secrets to Becoming a Successful DJ

If you have ever dreamed of being a DJ with people dancing to your music, all while having the time of your life, then this audiobook will show you how.

From the bedroom to the hottest clubs, to events and main-stage festivals. Whether you're a seasoned pro looking to enhance your current skills or a new, aspiring DJ looking to get started -

Whatever your level of experience, the wisdom in this audiobook is explosive, and it is an absolute must to skyrocketing your success as a DJ.

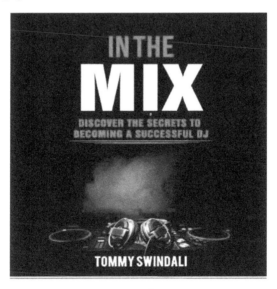

Discover "How to Find Your Sound"

http://musicprod.ontrapages.com/

Swindali music coaching/Skype lessons.

Email djswindali@gmail.com for info and pricing

Music Production: The Advanced Guide On How to Produce for Music Producers

Auto tune

Mid Side

Analyzer

Side Chaining

Be Minimal

Mastering

Preparation Stage

Enhancement Stage

Checking Stages

Conclusion / Finding Your Sound

The Power is in The People

No Excuses

Stop Waiting

Jump

Introduction

Maybe you are thinking about a career in music production or making some beats. But you see the mountain of knowledge you have to acquire in order to live out your dreams and it seems impossible to get to the level of your production superheroes. The reality is that what these superstar producers do is just like everybody else. They sit in front of their computer for many hours a day and a lot of the days they come up with nothing. If you're passionate about music like them and you're willing to stick at it then you will eventually produce some hot tracks. This book is here to help you acquire all of the required skills and knowledge.

So what exactly is a music producer? A music producer is to a musical recording as a director is to a movie. When it comes to making a movie there is a line drawn in other words the buck stops there at the director. Look at the director as the captain of the ship who controls and steers the ship working with everyone from the technical editors to the actors in order to achieve his or her overall vision of the movie. A music producer should be the exact same. They should control and have the technical expertise and skills to produce a hot track. Simply put a music producer provides the experience to create a polished work of art.

The first foundation of being a music producer is a knowledge of music theory and that has nothing to do with computers. Because of the super fast growth of computer tools such as vsts and virtual synthesizers people get caught up in the whole technical aspect of music when they really should focus on the songwriting aspect. Music theory, chords, melodies, harmonizing, voicing and all of that good stuff. You need to understand a little if you're going to make it. It is the ability to come up with musical arrangements that evoke certain emotions that will either make you want to jump up, party or sob and cry. I cannot emphasize enough how important music theory is, it is by far the most important skill set.

The next foundation is sound design because at the end of the day there are only a finite number of chord progressions that you can come up with. The difference is in the textures and the sounds that you use to convey these chord progressions and melodies. Beginners in sound design are what I'm going to call preset users. Many people will tell you that presets are no good. You're cheating if you're making music with presets and so on and so forth. The reality is that everybody started out with presets. Once you get more comfortable you can start to tweak presets which is the second category. You start out with presets and once you get a good idea going then you can start turning the knobs, add effects and modulate the sounds to make them more unique. At the end of the day most of your production heroes, the people who chart and play on the radio every day are probably either preset users or preset tweakers. Once you're comfortable tweaking presets then there's the third category which are sound designers. Look at some of the biggest names, these guys surely program some of their sounds but they also use presets and some of their own unique sounds are actually just presets that they tweaked a little bit differently.

Overall you have to know where you reside. Understanding your place will help you be comfortable with who you are, let you know what you're good at and then you can dive deeper. Later on you should consider learning the more technical aspects of music production such as mixing and mastering. If you're comfortable with sound design, then maybe you need to improve your songwriting skills and vice versa. If you look at the best producers out there they all have a good mixture of these two skill sets. If you look at the the Hollywood composing scene people like John Williams. Most of his scores use standard presets which are unaltered versions of orchestral instruments. On the other hand you have people like Hans Zimmer who compose fairly simple music but are so good at sound designing that they get most of the contracts on the biggest blockbusters. Then, if you look at hip-hop producers such as Mike Will Made It or or DJ Mustard they are preset users and their compositions are fairly simple. But the way that they put it all together and the particular presets that they pick make them sound very original. Finally, if you look at the EDM world you have very good sound designers such as Skrillex, Diplo and Deadmau5. There compositions are very original and pioneering due to the sounds they use which are often crafted by themselves.

Besides the foundations you need to have an overall vision for your music. This might come from a moment of inspiration or it could be something that happens when you really just sit and listen to your song and try to hear where it can go. What is it building to? What's the story you're telling? Listen to your favorite songs and do a lot of purposeful listening and learning around other people's music. Your first attempts will not be good. Getting stuck on one song for enormous amount of time will just hold you back. Move on quickly, try ideas, keep being creative, writing and recording. As your skill set grows you can always go back to those songs. No one creates at the highest levels all the time. If you sit there and wait for the creative juices to flow, believing that the only time you can work is when you feel creative will mean that nothing will get done. Regardless always create work through those times when you feel like you're not at your most creative. When you create things you will make mistakes and it is okay because you can learn from those mistakes. A lot of people are just getting a little bit too stressed and losing the fun in what they're doing. Before you know it all the music becomes too stressful and you're not in a very ideal or creative mindset to work. Often realizing that you're stressed can be quite difficult especially when you're working on something like music. If you're sitting away at the desk and you're frowning away and you're worried about it take a step back. Get out of the chair and get out of that area. Removing yourself from the environment can help you come up with different ways to overcome the problem. Then you can go back in and start working again. Try to spend as little time in the studio being stressed as possible so that you only associate sitting there with productive happy music.

Always keep developing and learning. You should be spending eighty percent of your time making music and twenty percent of your time going online finding tutorials and seeking out information. When you do seek out those tutorials seek them out for a specific purpose. Find relevant information and don't get caught into that trap of just watching endless amounts of everybody's opinion. The best way to retain information is for it to be purpose driven. You have a problem and you find a tutorial to solve it.

Finally, never compare yourself. When you see those superstar producers, you just see this rapid rise to fame. It seems like they're instantaneously successful and everyone knows who they are. But you don't see all the work that goes on behind the scenes. There's a one in a million person who's just brilliant right out the gate and the rest of us have to struggle, grow and create a lot of bad stuff. Maybe then some of that will be good and even then some of your stuff will still be bad. Often we can expect results a little bit too quickly.

Success in life that is truly worth having does take a long time to grow.

Embrace the journey, share ideas and be ready for the criticism you might take or the praise you might received. Music production is very much about the process and it's not just about the end goal of getting there and being successful. You need to enjoy the entire process, work your way through it and not get too hung up on wanting the success instantaneously. Given how fast everything moves these days it can be very easy to forget that skills take a long time to develop and there's nothing wrong with that. You should try to enjoy the process as much as possible.

Should You Study?

In the beginning of your music production journey you will need to spend more time on the learning just because there's so much that you need to get a foundational start. This leads to the question should you study music production? There are many institutes, colleges and universities offering really great course in music production.

Let's take a look at the advantages and disadvantages of enrolling to study. First, studying is a really good and easy way of meeting thousands of people. It sounds so cliche but it's so true. You genuinely won't get that experience sat in your bedroom no matter how many friends you may have at home. For example you might be a house music producer and you might need a singer on one of your tracks. If you're just sat at home you can maybe put up a Facebook post or have a look on some websites. But if you go to study, the likelihood is that one of your friends is going to be a singer. When you enrol to study you will be around a massive pool of production and performing talent that you can use which is so valuable. You can make relationships with these people, learn from them and start to make good music with them.

Next advantage is that studying music production is going to give you access to incredible equipment and facilities that you would normally not have access to without paying for. For example, normally you would never have the chance to mix on an SSL mixing desk or work in a studio with a control room with Pro Tools HD and a selection of professional microphones. Having the chance to get hands on experience working with that kind of stuff will help you determine whether it is something that you want to work in later on in life.

Next up the lecturers can be so so helpful in helping you to forge a career in music production. Criteria for lecturers is that they have to be actively participating in the industry to be able to lecture that subject at university. Therefore all of these lecturers are going to be people that have mixed and produced for bands that you will know. They're going to work for big companies that you will know and they're going to have really good connections. For you this could be very beneficial and open doors that otherwise wouldn't open. You could be an amazing mix engineer sat at home but if you don't know that guy that works for Universal Studios that can hook you up with a small band that needs a recording then you will be still sat at home.

Now the negatives. Studying is expensive, fees these days are on the rise and the only way that most students can afford them is with loans. The interest rates of these loans can be so high and they will keep on accumulating. Next, studying does not guarantee a job straight up after graduation because the industry is extremely competitive. However if you are going the extra mile, studying hard, working on projects outside of studies and making a name for yourself then it will give you a huge advantage. So many students go in with a minimal effort attitude and graduate with an average degree. Working hard will put you head and shoulders above the rest. Show up to the lectures and put in time and effort in outside of the lectures.

On a final note, almost all of the information in any course is available on the internet. This is going to be far less expensive and maybe quicker to access and digest. However you will require significant self discipline to follow through on that knowledge. Enrolling in a course will put you into a curriculum that will drive your progress forward. At the end of the day both studying at home and in a college or university have their own merits. The final decision based on your preferences and resources will be yours to make. The contents of this book should help you with your decisions in music production.

The Fundamentals of Music Production

Music Theory

Music theory is the backbone of producing great music. If you put regular time into learning and practicing it you will be rewarded so much in your creative journey.

As music producers we need an understanding of the fundamentals of music theory. We will go into music production techniques in more detail later on but for now let's get an understanding of the basic. The first step is knowing to how to find the notes on a piano. The music alphabet is the letters A through G and it just keeps repeating. When you look at the piano, you can see black keys and white keys. With the black keys you have groups of two and groups of three. The entire piano it's always groups of two and three. Now if you go to the first black key of a group of two and slide down to the left you have C. Now all you have to do is remember the alphabet C, D, E, F, G, A, B and you're back at C again. Then it keeps repeating on and on all the way up the scale.

The next thing I would advise you to learn is a key. The easiest keys to learn are C major and A minor. They use all of the white keys on the piano and by learning the key step by step you can easily figure out the chords that go with it. The A minor key starts on root note A and then uses all the following white keys until it cycles back around. The C major key starts with root note C and uses all the following white keys until it cycles back around. Major and minor keys are tools composers use to give their music a certain mood atmosphere or strength. Major and minor don't refer to single notes but to the spaces between notes and how far notes are from each other. These are measured in whole steps and half steps. Some combinations of whole and half steps create the sound of major and other combinations of whole and half steps create the sound of minor. Major usually sounds happy and triumphant. Whilst minor on the other hand often sounds bittersweet, sad and sometimes even scary. You can use each to its advantage depending on the emotion you are aiming to express through your music.

Now that you know some keys it's really easy to write melodies and chord progressions. Simply use only the keys in the scale. You can draw all of the notes in the scale into your DAW and mute them so you have a little guide. The easiest chord to use is the triad and it uses three keys. For most chords you would play the root note, skip one, play one, skip one and play one. So in the case of a C major triad you would use the keys C, E and G. You can add a seventh key on the top for extra harmony and create a seventh chord by adding the B. For the A minor triad use the keys A, C, E. To add the seventh use the key G. Another nice thing you can do is copying the root notes one octave down and you will get a chord that is a bit thicker. Maybe give them a slightly different rhythm to make it a bit more interesting. You can look up more chords online and try different variations in your music. Play the chords by ear and trust your instincts. To progress from chord to chord you can draw the root key in first and then try different variations on the top.

Once you have a good chord progression and bass line you can work on your melody. It doesn't necessarily have to be in this order. Music can start in any way. One of the simplest ways to write a melody is to first hum it. You can then get the rhythm of it correct by recording in your humming or drawing in notes on one key. Alternatively if you have a midi keyboard connected you could play it in. Next you need to tidy up the timing and then start to choose what keys you want each note to fall on. Make sure you stay within the scale of the key your working in and then it will be good to go. What I again suggest is to draw in all the notes of the scale and then mute them so you have a visual reference of what keys you can use. The melody should be consistent and catchy. Don't try to be too clever and switch it up all the time. Of course you want some variation to keep it interesting but maintain the essence of the song. Most popular music is very simple. A cool thing what many producers do is to shift the melody onto a different instrument. Listen to Calvin Harris songs, he does that a lot. Or check out some of the work of KSHMR who is great at switching up his melodies every few bars.

Science of Sound

As an aspiring music producer it's important to understand the fundamentals of how sound actually works. Figuratively speaking sound is a wave it, that is it's a vibration and travels through a medium such as air or water. Imagine if you drop a rock into a bucket of water it will disturb the surface of the water and create ripples or waves which travel away from the impact. The ripples cause the height of the water to change going up and down as the waves move away from the splash. These waves are visible with our eyes and have a number of properties. They have a maximum point called a crest and a minimum point called a trough. They have a wavelength which is the distance from a particular crest to the next one. They have an amplitude which is the distance from the top of a crest to the bottom of a trough. They have a frequency which is the number of waves that pass a fixed point per second.

In essence sound waves are similar. Imagine if you clap your hands in a quiet room it will disturb the air and cause ripples of air to move away from your hands. The clap disturbs the air molecules near your hands. These molecules then bounce into other nearby molecules and so on. The disturbance moves through the air like a wave in water. Sound waves create changes in air pressure causing particles to be bunched together or spread apart. There are not visible but our ears can hear them. When the waves reach our ears the air pressure goes up and down and this makes our eardrums go in and out in harmony. Our brain analyzes these signals and interprets them as sound.

Noise and notes are both a combination of sound waves at various different frequencies. The difference between them is that a note features a pattern of waves that repeats in an ordered way. Whilst a note consists of individual ripples that do not repeat and so are disordered. When an object moves it disturbs the surrounding air which will ripple out as sound waves. If the vibration of the object is fast with a repeating pattern then the sound waves will be more uniformly spaced and regular, like a string. The air particles will be squeezed together tightly into evenly spaced waves. To the ear these will be heard as notes with a distinct pitch. However if you hit a hammer on a surface you will hear a noise consisting of unrelated frequencies with no repeating pattern. To the ear this will be heard as a noise with no defined pitch.

As long as the pattern of waves repeats itself the sound produced will be a note regardless of how complicated the individual ripples are. Incidentally musical notes don't necessarily have be made by musical instruments. Anything that creates a vibration which disturbs the air in a uniform pattern will produce a note. For example the sounds of a Formula One race car engine or of a cat create a note. Smooth and even sound waves are created from instruments like a flute sound. Whilst more complex wave patterns that sound much richer are created by instrument like a violin.

Soundwaves generally have four main qualities. Frequency which determines the pitch, wave shape which determines the timbre, amplitude which determines the volume and phase which determines how sound waves interact. If a string vibrates back and forth two hundred times a second it's causing or emitting two hundred sound waves per second. The number of sound waves that pass a fixed point per second or the number of times a string vibrates per second is called the frequency and it is measured in hertz (hZ). If our string is vibrating at two hundred times per second then its frequency will be 200 Hertz. When you play middle A the frequency is 440 Hertz again this means the string is vibrating back and forth 440 times per second. Therefore frequency and wavelength determine the pitch of the sound.

Because all sound travels at the speed of sound which is roughly 343 m/s through air, waves with a shorter wavelength will arrive at our ears more frequently than longer waves. The pitch of a note is determined by its frequency. Changing the shape of the sound wave while keeping the same frequency will change how the note sounds and that is defined as its timbre. Sounds can have the same frequency but a different sound due to the wave being shaped differently / timbre. Wave shaping is done extensively in electronic music and this allows you to make a note sound much more interesting than a plain old boring sine wave.

The human ear can generally hear frequencies between 20 and 20,000 Hertz. Amplitude is a measurement of the amount of change in air pressure caused by a sound wave. It is a measure of the distance between the maximum and minimum of that wave and is measured in meters. All other things being equal if you increase the amplitude of the sound waves then you increase the volume of the sound. The perceived volume of the note depends on its frequency. Human hearing is more sensitive to notes in the middle range at around 2,000 to 5,000 Hertz. At the extreme bottom or extreme top of the range even when playing at the same amplitude a note will be perceived as quieter. This is why bass guitars or double basses always sound quieter than the rest of the band and while you hear the higher pitched instruments over the rest of the orchestra. Low-pitched instruments have to be played harder to get the same level of volume as higher pitched instruments. Keep this in mind when you are mixing.

The most common way of measuring loudness is with decibels. The decibel scale is used to compare the relative intensities of any two sounds. It is a measure of the intensity of a sound relative to the threshold of human hearing. Zero decibels is the softest level that a human can hear. The average level of speaking voices is around sixty decibels. Sounds above eighty five decibels can permanently damage your ears if you're exposed to them for a long time. Always wear inner ear protection if you are going to be exposed to loud sounds for a long period of time. Most ear damage is irreversible.

When you hit a piano key at first you will hear a loud ringing as the hammer hits the string and then there is an immediate fall in volume as the note is sustained. This variation of amplitude over time is referred to as the sound envelope. The sound envelope is made up of four parts. The attack which is the initial strike of the note which usually creates the loudest part of the sound. The decay which is the drop in intensity immediately after the attack. The sustain which is the steady-state sound of the note as it's sustained and the release which is when the key is released and the note stops sounding. The envelope of the sound helps determine an instrument. For example drums usually have a fast attack, decay, sustain and release. Whilst strings have a slow attack with longer decay, sustain and release times.

Digital Sound

The process of capturing sound in a digital format is called sampling. A sample is an aesthetic representation of a waveform in time. The amount of samples that are recorded per second is defined as sample rate. If we sample a twenty kilohertz frequency with a sample rate of twenty kilohertz the result will be one sample per completed cycle. In order to capture the full range of the cycle we need to have a sampling rate that is double the frequency that we're sampling. This is because when sampling, the highest frequencies can cause aliasing errors and various other problems. Therefore we need to filter off the highest frequencies with a low-pass filter. In order to compensate for the cut off we need to have a sample rate of at least forty kilohertz to properly capture a twenty kilohertz frequency.

We can say that sampling is the process of recording an amplitude value in time and it is captured during a process called quantization. Digital recording systems will capture samples at a specific resolution across the amplitude axis.

With a higher resolution the digital representation of the waveform will be much more accurate. The bit depth of the recording equipment being used will determine this. Having a higher bit depth will allow a greater dynamic range to be captured. A 16-bit recording has a theoretical dynamic range of 96 dB whereas 24 bit audio has a theoretical dynamic range of 144 dB. Mixing with the higher bit depth is great for recording very dynamic sources such as an orchestra which can go from very quiet to very loud in its dynamic range. Audio interfaces nowadays can support sampling rates of up to 192 kilohertz for much higher audio quality and processing options.

The filters and the analogue to digital converters that are being used by an audio interface are really crucial in determining what the quality of the recorded audio will be. Having a higher bit depth will make mixing processing more accurate and also offer a lot higher resolution when using effects such as EQ, reverb, compression, etc. Everything will sound much better at the higher sample rate. In fact, many plugins feature up sampling techniques to internally work at higher sample rates. Higher sample rates however will stress your computer a lot more so you'll definitely need some more processing power. If you don't have that keep in mind that you won't be able to add as many tracks or plugins as you were used to at lower sample rates.

Build Your Dream Studio: Computer Music

Building a studio might seem unrealistic when you think of those big studios used by the professionals. You might think that achieving the same results that you would in a full fledged professional studio is near impossible. However with the fast development power of the modern producing world it is becoming easier than ever to make high quality music from your home studio. The key to building your first studio is to always utilize what you have. It isn't necessarily about having the very best equipment but rather knowing how to use what you have effectively. If your on a budget you can still get great equipment at an affordable price. Know what your budget is and then it's up to you to allocate your money appropriately. Let's take a look at what equipment you need to set up your first studio.

A word of warning first. One of the major problems that we have in the modern home recording era is that there is so much gear available. This is a great blessing but the curse of it is there's so much available that we think that there's something better out there and that we should be using everybody's using different gear. We watch an interview with our favorite producer and we say man they use those plugins or those monitors I got to get those. There's nothing wrong with wanting to use the gear that your friends or your heroes or whatever use. The problem is is when we always change our gear so often we never get to really learn it. We never get to really master our gear, we never really get to learn the nuances and the details of what our gear can do. If you keep changing your tools your going to keep going back to learning now you're not thinking about music making. Get something commit to it, use it and make a lot of music with it.

Computer

The first piece of equipment you will need is a computer. I'm not going to get into the Mac versus PC discussion because both offer really great options. Today's computers can handle so much more and I'm sure that what you have is perfectly fine to get started.

If you don't really need to or plan to travel with your computer often then always choose a desktop computer. For the price and speed a desktop computer will be a much better option. In order to fit the components of a laptop into that small space manufactures make compromises. Whatever you decide on the fundamental things to look out for are the same.

Some of the things you should look out for are ram, hard drive space and fast, reliable processors. For the processor choose an i7 or if you have the budget an i9. The best manufacturer and one you should always go with is an Intel processor. For ram/memory, 8gb would be the starting point and if you can afford to choose 16gb. Although in most computers you will always have the option to upgrade the memory later on. When selecting a hard drive make sure that you have one that is fast enough to handle reading multiple tracks at the same time. Ideally you need to have at least 7200 rpm or better even a SSD which will also save on the battery life of your laptop. In addition make sure that you have enough hard disk space with 500gb being the bear minimum. Even one terabyte of space still isn't really adequate because you will run out of space eventually so try to go above that. Also you should regularly back up your data to an external hard drive. For your screen preferably go for a 17-inch and if you have an external monitor you can hook that up via HDMI which is great for having one screen for mixing and another for arrangement. Also make sure that you have a backlit keyboard so you can easily see your keyboard in low lighting which is in most studios.

Apple with their MacBook series offer extended warranty and are known for using quality components that last long and are durable. When something is broken they can probably fix it quite easily and also they still work great over five years on from buy date. Acer, Lenovo and Samsung have some gaming laptops that are designed to withstand heavy workloads and that's good for music production. Take in mind the specifications outlined and see what is available for your budget. Be sure to also research any computer thoroughly and check out all the reviews before you invest.

Software

Next up you will need some software or Digital Audio Workstation (DAW). This will be your command center and it is where all your recordings will go and is where you work on your music. There are a lot of options out there. Now if you're running a Mac this decision is very simple, start with GarageBand. It's a free software that will familiarize you with recording, mixing and producing. There are many more different Digital Audio Workstations out there and I will cover the bigger ones here. Overall the best DAW is the one that you can work the quickest and be the most comfortable with. Don't listen to what everybody else says, that you need to use Ableton or Logic or whatever. Every DAW has its own strengths and weaknesses and if there was one DAW for everybody then everybody would use it. If your not sure you can download a demo of one of the DAW's and test it out before you buy.

Pro Tools

Pro Tools is still regarded as the industry standard digital audio workstation at the moment so if you're looking for the best of the best then this is definitely it. The majority of professional recording studios are using it so if you have some type of knowledge of it then that's a great advantage to have because it will make your future studio experiences a lot more easier.

It is well known for rendering great quality audio and is a seamless choice for large recordings of instruments. It's also got 64-bit architecture which means that it will take advantage of any of your computer's RAM / 4 gigabyte as well and it's Windows and Mac compatible so it doesn't matter what computer you have.

Pro Tools is definitely aimed at professional there's number of reasons for this and the first is that there's a very limited number of stock plugins. This is intentional because they're expecting that people are going to have their own third-party plugins and hardware that are used in a traditional analog studio. However it does support most third party plugins and integrates easily with hardware recording equipment. The stock plugins that come with it are exceptional, they're very high quality and sound great. The software is very user customizable, you can change a lot of the parameters to your taste and what you like to see on a daily basis. Large studios particularly only use Pro Tools for tracking bands and mixing but there are still many composers that use it for songwriting.

Currently it is on version 12 and the is available as a monthly subscription of $25 per month for one year or for one payment of $299. Famous users include, Timbaland, Dr Dre, Paul Epworth, Pharrell Williams and many more.

Logic Pro X

Logic Pro X has come on the scene as being a real heavy hitter for electronic music producers and even producers that are working with bands. If you're upgrading from GarageBand, Logic is a very natural progression. Building on the basics of GarageBand it is a fully featured DAW that can do just about everything Pro Tools and every other DAW does. You get full multitrack mixing and you can insert all the plugins you want. Plus there's a 64-bit application to support audio unit plugins at 64 bit rates. The interface is really to navigate, for the singer-songwriter especially and that makes it really easy to make music.

The stock plugins are really great. In particular the amps and pedals which model the features of real amps and sound great. For singers the flex pitch is a great stock plug in which allows you to fix the pitch and timing of any audio. A very unique virtual drummer takes the concept of virtual drums to be even more user-friendly inside the DAW application. You can choose the kit you want and build it and customize it to be loud, soft whatever you want. Then you've got plenty of loops ordered in different sound types, instruments, key and bpm.

At the moment Logic Pro X is exclusively only available for Mac. The price point of Logic Pro X is around $199 which is super reasonable for what you're getting from the software. Famous users include, Hardwell, Calvin Harris, Swedish House Mafia, Alesso and many more.

Ableton Live

Ableton Live offers seamless music production and excellent onboard plugins. It really sets itself apart with the algorithms it uses to manipulate sound in general. Whether you're into sound design, composition work, production for bands or something a little more outside of the box then your options with Ableton really are unlimited.

The concept of collections to the browser is a great user friendly option to pull together all of your favorite sounds, samples, presets, plugins and projects all into one place. The new capture function allows you to easily save performances even if you weren't recording at the time which makes it really easy to capture spontaneity. You can play loops along with your session and quickly scroll through them as they will be played in BPM with the rest of the session. This is very practical if you're hunting for loops and trying to build your dance groove within your arrangement. You can also create quite complex mixing structures.

The stock plug ins are really high quality, you can create very digital sounds or very analog style sounds. Or you can create really warm smooth sounds or really aggressive sounds, it's all very diverse. They have several different analog distortion boxes from a warm crisp overdrive sound to a modern aggressive distortion and much more. Then there are a bunch of different delay devices from analogue tape delay to digital hardware delay. There are many more great stock plug ins to explore inside, just dive in they are really user friendly.

Ableton is really popular with EDM producers and from a live standpoint it is unreal the things that you can do it. It reacts really well with CPU intensive plugins and it still manages to keep a low latency most of the times. The full version rounds out at about $229. There are also lite version available for a cheaper price. Famous users include, Flume, Skirllex, Diplo, Bauuer and many more.

Fl Studio

Fl Studio started out under the name fruity loops and they released in 2018 a Mac version so it's now available on Windows and on the Mac. FL Studio has a little bit of an image problem. A lot of people don't take FL Studio seriously because it looks different to a lot of other DAW'S. Some might say it looks a little bit basic or amatuer. But don't mistake it's look for the power it possesses.

The interface is really user friendly and has some powerful tools. The pattern roll is a really cool feature which allows you to quickly program in a complete drum loop. Normally this could take you hours of time spent editing in the piano roll or otherwise trying to record your loops in live. If your computer is low on RAM the step editing mode lets you input notes by a computer keyboard or MIDI without having to record anything live which significantly reduces MIDI latency.

FL studio comes with a great set of stock plugins that can be used for mixing, engineering and mastering your music. With these you will easily be able to achieve very professional sounding music results. There are more than enough included to cater for your requirements without having to invest more cash in buying other unnecessary plug-ins. Then there are the virtual synthesizers which include subtractive, additive, drum, granular and even frequency modulation. These are great for giving you the opportunity to create unique sounds in a variety of music genres.

One of the greatest things about FL Studio is that it comes with a variety of different sample packs that you can use to program strings, choirs, brass, woodwinds and many more different types of instruments. The browser window also makes them extremely easy to preview. All you have to do is click the sample file with your mouse and you'll get a preview of the sound. This makes searching for the perfect kick or snare sound a smooth and effortless process. Finally the sample editor is an awesome tool for those of you who want to produce glitch music or music with a lot of edits in. This will save you literally hours of time from manually cutting stretching and pitching audio files. It really is a powerful feature and you can hear it in a lot songs that have these pitch chop vocal drops.

The price of FL Studio starts at $199 for the basic package and upto $899 for the full package with all plugins and synthesizers. Famous users include, Martin Garrix, Porter Robinson, Afrojack and many more.

Reason

Reason by Propellerheads has a great sound design engine that lets you easily combine many instruments to create amazing sounds from the stock sounds. Some of your favorite songs are probably made from stock Reason sounds. The user interface is really easy to use with customizable options and great performance. Writing songs and drawing in automation is a breeze.

Inside it has some really great synths. Europa is a really awesome and incredibly powerful modern synth that uses almost no processor power. The vocal synth is excellent at choir type effects and then clanging the tuned percussion is awesome. The piano is fantastic and the samplers inside make it really easy for adding in other sample instruments. You can of course combine all those instruments together to create really cool and unique sounds. It uses hardly any processing power to do that. Also if you want you can run Reason in the background of another DAW so it becomes almost like this epice VST. In addition to the stock sounds Reason 10 provides full VST support.

The price of reason is currently $299 with the option of a free trial for thirty days. Famous users include, DJ Mustard, Mike Will Made It, The Prodigy and many more.

Plug Ins and Virtual Synthesizers

Plug ins and virtual synthesizers are made by third party developers to be used in your chosen DAW. Most DAW's will also have their own stock plugins and synths for standard things such as compression, EQ, reverb, chorus, panning, etc. There are so many different kinds of plug ins that can be used to change, enhance or fix the sound. Adding some to your collection will give you more power. But before you do that make sure your buying it for the right reasons. Don't get the latest plug in because it is hot now. If the stock plug in does the job then stick with it. Anway, let's take a look at some of the most popular plug ins.

Waves
Waves are currently one of the most famous and respected developers of plug ins and signal processors in the music production industry. So many of the world's top producers are using them. They are known and well respected for very high quality and are used in every aspect of music production from mixing and mastering to production, live sound and more.

They are particularly well known for reverb, compression, EQ, limiting, noise reduction. The quality does come at a price but there are many different bundles available to cater for your requirements. For compatibility they offer versions in VST, TDM, RTAS and AU formats,

Izoptope

Izotope are well respected in the music production industry as offering great sound to help producers and engineers seamlessly improve their music. They have designed award winning software and plugins. Ozone 8 is one of their most popular plugins. It is a full mastering suite with intelligent signal processing, signal shaping, tone balancing and more. It aims to provide the user with a full set of mastering tools and can be used in RTAS, AAX, VST, AU or as a stand alone unit.

Another of their popular plugins is Izotope Trash. This is one of the most advanced distortion units available. It can combine powerful, multi band, dual stage and filtered distortion units. This will give warmth, crunch or hardcore distortion to your sounds. Highly recommend for guitars and drums.

Fabfilter

Offer plugins for reverb, EQ, compression, mid side, limiting and more. Known for being user friendly and having high fidelity output. Powerful and innovative. They are available to try out in demo version first and buy late if you like. www.splice.com also offer rent to own options.

Valhalla Room

A clean and realistic reverb. Features twelve reverb algorithms that produce a variety of natural reverberation sounds. Sounds range from light ambience in rooms to huge halls and vast spaces. All algorithms can be altered to the users preferences.

Guitar Rig

Guitar Rig is plug in used to model amplifiers and effects from guitar pedals. It is primarily aimed to be used with guitars and basses but can work well with various other signal inputs. Very user friendly and offers a lot of different combinations to produce really cool sounds.

Melodyne

Celemony Melodyne is an excellent plug in used for changing and correcting the pitch of sounds. Typically this is used on vocals but could be used on other pitched instruments. For example if you recorded in a vocal and there are some notes that are a bit off key or off time then you can easily fix that with Melodyne. This also works on chords as well as single notes. It is very transparent and can turn an out of tune vocal into a pitch perfect one. However it makes life easier if the original vocal is well performed and recorded in the first place. Supported in VST, AU and stand alone units.

Sugar Bytes Effectrix

Sugar Bytes Effectrix is a multi effects plug in used for sequenced sound manipulations. It allows you to mash up or tweek your beats, create new patterns, reverse, stretch, delay and alter your sounds in upto sixteen different ways.

VSTIS

Virtual studio instruments (VSTIS) allow you to add in powerful software instruments into your DAW. This will allow you to utilize anything from modern synthesizers to real world instruments. All DAW's will come with a few stock DAW's but these are usually quite basic compared to what is out there. Let's take a look at some of the best ones.

Komplete

Brings all of the Native Instruments, instrument and effect plugins together into one comprehensive package ready to run as a standalone instrument or inside the DAW of your choice. Offers a huge library of synthesizers, sampled instruments and expansion packs with over 25,000 preset sounds and fifty instruments/processors. This really is a solution to every aspect of sound and includes the following. Kontakt, an award winning sampler which is great for loading drum hits and multi samples to create your own instruments. There are also excellent sound libraries offered with this. You got pianos, strings, basses, drums, orchestras and more all at your fingertips. Massive, a very popular synthesizer which can easily create digital and analogue style sounds. Reaktor which allows you to program in your own instruments and effects, endless possibilities. Guitar Rig Pro, used for awesome guitar style effects. Maschine, a drum creation and programming tool. FM8 advanced FM synthesizer and much more. Also included in the package is a hardware keyboard controller.

Serum

Serum is a groundbreaking virtual synthesizer that has become an industry standard in the music production world. If you are in any way into sound design and all that stuff this is hands down one of the best synthesizers you can get for the money. The quality of the sound is unbelievable. It has your basic oscillators to create the wave table sounds and you can also drag and drop any sound into the oscillators. Plus you have a sub oscillator for your bass and a noise oscillator so you can add some external noise. These will both help to fill out your sounds. The filter options are really great with so many different types available. You can filter, add envelopes, lfos, effects and much more. The matrix routing options are really powerful. Included are a lot of high quality presets that you can easily access across different categories. The sounds that are included are really great or you can easily make your own from scratch or just work on the existing ones.

Sylenth

Sylenth is a really popular virtual synthesizer that is used by many of the biggest names in music production. It's good for pads, leads, arpeggiators, baselines and more. The interface is really flexible and allows you to easily adjust sounds and parameters. You can route things really easy, for example to set up lfo's or envelope modulations. It also comes with a built in compressor, reverb, delays, equalizer, chorus, phase and distortion. I highly recommend this if you want to start producing electronic music because you will get some great sounds out of it.

Nexus

Nexus is a really powerful Rom sampler with some amazing sounds and has the option for adding on sound banks from famous producers. It features an extremely efficient screen which by default displays the different sound banks and all of the presets inside of them. This makes it easy to find the sound you are looking for.
On the interface are six main sections, the first section is the filter modifier and this section includes the envelope cutoff and resonance along with the standard ADSR envelopes. There is a master filter which can control the master cutoff and resonance of the sound. Controlling these knobs along with

automation is a great way to add flavor to any track. Nexus also includes its own effects units which are delay and reverb. The quality of these are quite high nice so you don't have to worry about adding another plugin to your mixer channel. Additional tabs include the modulation arpeggiator and trance gate. The standard version comes with many great presets or you can add expansion packs.

Spire

Spire is a virtual synthesizer that has a really powerful sound and works well in dance music and hip hop. It comes with five banks and you can also get more packs online or creating your own sounds is very easy. There are four oscillators which have numerous wavetables available to be detuned, mashed and smashed together in harmony. Then there are some awesome filters with a multitude of different ones available for filtering your sounds. The effects section has five effects including shaping, phase, chorus, delay and reverb. These are really great and you probably won't need any extra plug ins. Finally, the routing options of are excellent and overall the synth is super easy to use and produces great sounds.

Omnisphere

Omnisphere is a virtual instrument that has both a huge synth engine as well as an enormous bank of sampled sounds. It has almost endless sound design capabilities and therefore it is great for composers and sound designers but really it can be used for any style of music. It comes with a vast library of over 12,000 sounds in almost every kind of style from EDM to soundscapes. It is also very easy to either create your own sounds from scratch or make variations on any of the included patches. You can choose how deep you want to go in your own sound design you can use the easy interface for fast workflow or go deep into custom modulation. If you invest in it you will want a powerful computer with a large hard drive because it is demanding in space and performance.

Build Your Dream Studio: Hardware

Audio Interface

In order to send the sounds from your computer to speakers or headphones and also to convert the analogue signal from your microphone or instrument your going to need an audio interface. Personally I use an Apogee duet as my main audio interface but there's just so many great options out there. Universal Audio is a big favorite but I think the best option for those of you who are starting out is the Scarlett Solo from Focusrite. It's $99 and it comes with two free software options, Pro Tools or Ableton Live Lite. It features one microphone input and one instrument input and it records at really high sample rates which will be perfect for your home studio recording needs.

Headphones

Next you will need a set of headphones. Medium priced headphones will be fine, you don't necessarily need the most expensive headphones. I recommend you visit a professional audio store and test out a few different sets there based on your budget. Also take a look at the reviews of them before you invest. To help you more,check out the top five best studio headphones that I recommend. These are based on their price, quality, durability and more.

Sony MDR 75006

The Sony MDR 75006 have been around in the industry for a little while which make them a trusted and certified option for the music producer who is looking for strong, lasting and quality headphones. From a design perspective these headphones are closed off at the back so you will barely notice any external noise interference. In turn this will help you to be more focused on your music. They come in an all black finish with a comfortable, padded headband that sits softly on your head. This helps them to stay on your head whilst ensuring a higher level of comfort. Storing them in the included soft case is really easy because the ear cups are also foldable and so you can maintain their original look. The cable attachment is extremely long and durable so you can still be quite mobile. The MDR 75006 have been greatly praised for their ability to output a well matched audio from the left and the right drivers. This is really important because you can feel an accurate localization and enjoy having a better stereo image.

Audio Technica ATHM70X

The audio technica ATHM70X are closed-back professional studio monitor headphones that combine a reasonable price with a really strong performance. From a design perspective these headphones feature a stylish all-black well-built construction that consists of 90 degree swiveling ear cups and a sturdy plastic headband that is wrapped in a soft material. This will reduce pressure points on your head so you won't feel tight. Included with them are three detachable cables including a coiled cable, two straight cables and a 1/4 inch screw on an adapter plus a carrying case as well so you will be equipped with everything needed. The sound quality is exceptionally balanced in the lows and highs. They also have an excellent sound isolation. Since these headphones have a fold flat design it means that you won't have any difficulties in terms of portability and storage.

BeyerDynamic DT 1990 Pro

The BeyerDynamic DT 1990 Pro are among one of the most popular studio headphones in the music production industry. In fact you have probably seen this model come up many times if you were searching for headphones. From a design perspective they feature an open back all black or all grey construction that is made of strong metal that is cased in padding / foam. This make them both long lasting and very comfortable. Both the headband and the ear sets can be easily replaced. This is great since most headphones don't have that option. Included are also two pairs of cables that are a straight cable and a coiled cable along with a strong, hard case to offer a secure storage. The sound produced is very detailed and accurate from the left and the right stereo field. Many users have also stated that the low end is really well defined, whilst the mids and highs are very well produced as well. However the isolation isn't quite as good since they have an open design that is primarily designed for mixes and mastering. But this is quite normal and won't be a setback.

Bowers & Wilkins P9

The Bowers & Wilkins P9 is an excellent option for music production headphones. From a design they look really cool and are set in an aluminum frame with real leather headband and ear cups. This gives them an expensive look and also feels extremely comfortable on your head. Adjusting them and finding an ideal position is very easy and they will lock in place allowing you to wear them for long periods of time without feeling discomfort. They come with a detachable four foot cable, remote and an really long cable for listening at home. Regarding sound quality they do an excellent job in producing an accurate representation with clarity and would never disappoint with their performance. Overall they look both as good as they perform.

Sennheiser HD 800 S

The Sennheiser HD 800 S are premium headphones which are great for music producers who want to invest in a pair of headphones that are armed with everything required. From a design perspective they feature an open back design that is made of strong metal and comfortable padding. The headband is covered with several layers of resonance damping polymers that play a crucial role in minimizing vibrations. This basically means that they will absorb any unwanted resonance energy while enhancing the high and the low frequency range so the end result will be of a very high quality. They come with two cables including a four pin XLR balanced cable that will provide a better audio quality from sources with balanced outputs. Sound performance wise they have a full detailed sound with minimal distortion. Give them a try and assure yourself that they have great quality.

Speakers

If you decide to use speakers instead of headphones than that is a good idea because you will be able to listen to a more accurate representation of the audio. Speakers can produce lower frequencies more accurately and are reproducing audio in a three dimensional plane. It is a good idea to use a combination of speakers and headphones. You want to always be testing your mixes on both and then striking a balance between the two. This will help your mixes to translate well across the different systems. Also in some situations your room or lifestyle might limit your options. For example maybe you travel a lot. In this situation i would advise you to produce most of your music with headphones and then at the mixing and sound design stages you can move over to speakers. Now, let's take a look at the top five best studio monitors

Mackie CR 3

The Mackie CR 3 is a pair of compact studio monitors that combine excellent audio quality for an affordable price. From a design perspective they feature a wooden construction that is finished with a green and black color combination which looks very stylish. Regardless of where you put them they will look good. The speakers can output fifty watts of power whilst the audio frequency response ranges from 80 to 20 kilohertz. They come with a number of accessories which allows you to connect a computer, smartphone or media player. Another great thing about these speakers is that they come with isolation pads which will drastically minimize the build-up of any boomy low frequencies and enhance your overall listening focus.

M-Audio AV 42

The M-Audio AV 42 are an ideal option for most small home studios. From a design perspective they feature a compact construction that is mostly made of MDF and this cuts weight drastically. In addition they have a black matte finish which makes them very look stylish indeed. They can be connected to most of your gear including, tablets, computers and mixers. The frequency response is from 75 to 20,000 Hertz and the four inch woofer will reproduce a great amount of bass so you can feel every audio track in depth. Overall they produce great quality audio and will never restrict you in terms of connectivity.

Yamaha HS 8
The Yamaha HS 8 have quickly become a first choice of speaker for most professional music studios. From a design perspective they feature an attractive sleek white MDF design. On the speakers are controls that include room control and high frequency trim. The room control switch helps to compensate for the build up of low end frequencies which can cause exaggeration. This usually happens if you've placed the speakers to close to walls or in the corners. Whilst the mid and high trim help to tame excess high frequency build up which is common in most home studios. Included you can find one XLR and a 1/4 inch TRS phone jack input that can accept both balanced or unbalanced signals. The amplifier unit will ensure that each speaker delivers a high-resolution sound as well as a flat response across your entire room. They also have a noise reduction technology which results in effective reduction of noise by up to six decibels.

KRK Rokit 5
The KRK Rokit are a great set of speakers from KRK systems at an affordable price. They have a number of different sized models but the five inch speaker is going to be perfect for most people. If you need more low end response, the addition of subwoofers can help. From a design perspective they come in a really, solid design with a smooth contour. On the back of the speakers are a main volume knob for setting output level without having to overloaded the mixer. Also then you have a

high frequency level adjustment knob which is pretty common in speakers. This will help to compensate rooms that cause excess high frequency build up. You might notice this when you mix. Things will sound crisp and bright punchy but when you take the mix outside of that room it sounds muffled. Using a control like this allows you to cut out some of the high frequencies because your room is giving you more high frequencies than you need. The speakers feature standard RCA connections and balanced TRS connections which can connect to a variety of equipment types. These speakers are self powered / active monitors so you can just plug them straight into the wall. Overall they produce a high quality and accurate sound for an affordable price.

Midi Keyboard

If your good at piano or you want to be able to perform your own melodies then a midi keyboard is the best way to record your ideas into your DAW. Just plug it into your computer via USB cable or through a midi interface. Most audio interfaces have midi capability but if not it is easy to get a decent midi connector for an affordable price. Signals sent from the keyboard will tell the computer what notes are being pressed. In most DAW's you can adjust how responsive the keyboard is. For keyboards I recommend models from M-audio or Native Instruments. You can choose the keys to be semi weighted or fully weighted. The latter is more expensive but will feel much more like a piano and be easier to play. In addition if you want to control other parameters in your DAW you can use a midi controller such as a beatpad. Ableton have a really awesome step controller which allows you to assign various parameters to the grid buttons. This is really powerful for performances or recording in automation movements.

Microphone

If your recording instruments or vocals you will need a microphone. Now let's say you're a singer or recording vocals and the quality of vocals is really important to you. If this is the case well then you need to understand the different types of microphones that are available. Most will fit into one of three different categories, ribbon microphones, condenser microphones or dynamic microphones. Ribbon microphones are more rare and you are less likely to see them and much less likely to afford them. Condenser microphones are the best for high quality studio recordings. They are incredibly sensitive to sources and produce accurate results and are particularly good in the high frequencies. In the majority of situations condenser microphones will reproduce a better quality of recording than a dynamic microphone would. Dynamic microphones are more durable and less sensitive therefore making them more suitable for live performances. However this is not to say that dynamic microphones are only useful for live music. In fact the Shure SM57 is probably one of the most used microphones for music recordings. But in a lot of cases especially when recording vocals you're going to want a good condenser microphone.

The price of condenser microphones can get astronomically high. But don't worry, you don't have to break the bank to get something decent. For under $200 the Bluebird from Blue Microphones offers great sound quality. As your studio evolves and you start adding things like preamps this microphone is only going to become more powerful. Another great budget option is the Samson CO1. Now if you know a little bit about condenser microphones you will surely of heard of the Neuman U87. It is widely regarded as one of the best microphones that money can buy. It is expensive but for the price you will get value for money. The sound quality is high and high frequencies are particularly well produced. This makes it a great microphone for recording acoustic guitars or as a drum overhead mic or even just a general room microphone. In addition it is also a favourite for recording with vocals.

Other options are the Audio Technica models who have a great range of condenser microphones that have a lot of similarities to the Neuman U87. In addition the Audio Technica series offers a couple of advanced features which make their application very multi-purpose. First of all they have multi patterned microphones which simply put means that there are a few different settings that determine how the microphone picks up sound. It can be an omnidirectional pattern, a cardioid pattern and a bi-directional pattern which basically just adds to the versatility of the microphones.

Last but not least it's worth mentioning again the Sure SM57 and Shure SM58. Yes, these are dynamic microphones but they are incredibly popular because they are both durable and produce high quality results. The SM57 is usually used for female vocals and higher frequency sounds whilst the SM58 is usually used for male vocals and lower frequency sounds. If you are looking for a great bass drum microphone the Shure Egg drum microphone is an excellent choice. In addition these microphones will work well in the studio and on the live stage. Shure microphones are going to last for a long time, produce great results and won't break the bank.

With your microphones you will want to get a couple of accessories including a mic stand, XLR cables and a pop filter. Always use XLR cables, they are balanced which means there will be less noise. In addition invest in high quality cables, it's no use having a decent microphone with a rubbish cable. The pop filter is going to help protect the microphone from popping sounds that are created by P and S sounds. You can also add in a sound shield or an acoustic shield will help to eliminate sound from bouncing off other surfaces in your room and traveling into the microphone. This offers a more affordable and easier solution to sound treating a room with acoustic treatment and bass traps. It simply sits behind the microphone.

Hey, I hope you're enjoying this book....if so please share your feedback with a good review.

Acoustic Treatment

If you do decide to treat your room then you can look into acoustic treatment solutions. Often you will find that when you play back your mixes in your home studio that it doesn't sound quite right. You fiddle with the settings in the mix thinking it might be that but it's to no avail. You might think to blame your studio monitors themselves or the microphone you used to record. But often times in a home recording studio that's not the real issue you're dealing with. In many cases the culprit is sound reflections.

When sound travels and bounces off a surface it ultimately affects the way you hear it. As a home recording music producer you're probably working in less than ideal conditions. Any flat walls, ceilings, hardwood or tiled floors and countertops can all be reflective surfaces which sound waves will bounce off of making the audio you hear have reflections. If your recording in any square or rectangular room with parallel walls, similar to the rooms in most people's houses then your playback is at the risk of comb filtering. When two or more sound waves reflect off of a surface and crash into each other it causes a delay. That may sound like a cool idea but it actually affects the way you hear the audio. As the sound waves wind up hitting your ears at different times they also hit each other at the wrong time causing interference and cancelation. This can cause your music to sound weak or muddled but it is most likely just an effect of the room you're working in and not necessarily your mixing technique.

Absorption and Diffusion
So if something as basic as parallel walls is affecting your mixing how do you change it? No one expects you to remodel

your house, a much easier solution is acoustic treatment. To start with there are two types of acoustic treatment to consider when thinking about your space, absorption and diffusion. With absorption sound waves become absorbed and are unable to reflect off the walls. Whereas diffusion breaks up the sound waves before they can collide with each other. For now let's talk about absorption. That's the option most people think of when talking about acoustic treatment. We've all seen photos of professional recording studios with the foam panels on the wall. Absorbing sound before it has a chance to reflect off the walls will eliminate a lot of the problems with those unwanted reflections. The best way to absorb the sound is with absorption panels. Absorption panels can be found in many styles but you'll often find them composed of polyurethane foam or fiberglass. They either come as a tile or a brick of foam or as one of the absorptive materials mentioned that is then wrapped in cloth fabric. These are generally several inches thick as the density of the material is important for the absorption and dampening of the sound waves. Now, some people might assume that any sort of foam will do the trick and some do-it-yourself websites suggest using material like a foam mattress topper or the egg crate stuff. However these materials are far too thin, after all it's meant for comfort and is not dense enough to properly absorb sound. Plus generally they will look very ugly.

When placing proper absorption panels around your home studio generally you'll want to situate them at ear level on each wall of the room. These should be at your early reflection points because the monitors should be pointed at your ears to allow you to hear the best audio mix. The sound waves especially the high frequency audio waves will travel out in that direction to your walls and reflect back to your ears causing you to hear the sound waves more than once. By placing absorption panels in these locations you stop that reflection from happening because as the sound that reaches those walls will be absorbed. This helps you to only hear the audio signal as it is coming out of your monitors.

A good way to judge the exact right spot for those absorption pales is with a help from a friend in your home studio. Sit in your chair and have the monitors facing your ears. Have a friend stand against one wall with a mirror and move back and forth along it. Now turn your head or your body towards your friend and follow the mirror. Most likely if you can see the face of the monitor in the mirrors reflection you're going to get an audio reflection in that spot so put some absorption paneling there. Other good places to put absorption panels are the wall directly behind you, the ceiling right above your seat and right behind the monitors themselves. Also having a carpeted floor or placing a throw rug on the floor can help dampen some of those sound waves.

Now you may be thinking, why not use absorption panels over the whole room just to be safe? While that may sound like a good idea in theory that will actually dull the natural acoustics of the room and leave your audio sounding bland. Some say covering about fifty percent of the walls should do the trick however in most home recording studios thirty to forty percent should work just fine. The goal for a home recording studio isn't necessarily a perfect setup it's just improving it as much as you can. Something is better than nothing. However if your budget does allow for fifty percent coverage then go for it.

The other less common option for reducing reflections throughout a home studio is diffusion. Diffusers are mathematically uneven and irregularly shaped surfaces or cabinets with varying depths that allow the audio waves to bounce around and break out without colliding or interfering with each other. This allows the audio waves to scatter so you'd still be able to hear them but with the reduced intensity. That's instead of letting the audio get absorbed. This retains the live ambiance of the sound without an echo. Mostly you will see those in high-end professional studios that can afford them.

Bass Traps

The absorption and diffusion panels will help with those mid and high frequency early reflection. Low end frequencies like those produced from a bass sound can cause their own issues. Luckily there is a solution to that as well. Bass traps, these are generally blocks of foam molded to fit in the corners of a room. They stop low end frequencies from reflecting in those corner areas where they tend to bunch up. Without bass traps there's a high chance of noise cancellation which could make it sound like you are lacking that low end power. Conversely depending on how close you and your monitors are to the corners of your room it could have the opposite effect and sound like you have more bass than you actually do.

Producing Music

It is really easy to start producing your first songs and most DAW's allow you to create a song using mostly software instruments. If you wanted to plug a microphone in or plug in an instrument you can do that too. The realm of creative possibilities are endless.

Before you get started producing music you should remove all creative distractions. Put your phone on silent, turn off the wifi and block off some time. The general atmosphere of a workspace is important. You should want to spend time in there, it should feel comfortable, organization goes a long way. The quicker and better you are, the more time you can spend making music. Learn shortcuts and inner working of whatever you're working with. This will lead to a smooth and seamless workflow

Get inspired and train your musical instincts. Put on your favorite records and analyze the living hell out of them. Listen to each individual instrument. Where is the instrument placed in the soundscape? How loud is it? What kind of effects does it have on it? What kind of feeling does the song evoke? The more you are studying and thinking about this stuff the more you can pick up the elements you like or dislike. You can then add those elements to your music or make sure you avoid them.

When you are producing music, try to focus on the project you're working on and not to work on ten projects at the same time. Because if you're doing the arrangement on one track and then doing it on four or five other tracks when get back to one of them you will kind of forgot where you are. Stick with it and try to finish it in one go. I know it's not always possible. Sometimes you get stuck and you just want to move on. In some cases you can just leave it for a while, let it simmer. Work on something else and then come back with a fresh perspective. Maybe you end up making some huge changes and it becomes a great song. Overall you should aim to finish thing quickly, any mistakes you made can be learned and applied to the next song.

Melody and Chords

There are a number of ways to start a song. Maybe it's a vocal, an idea or a sound. One of the best ways to start a song is with a melody. When it comes to creating the melody, think of a rhythm first and hum it out. You can then record that into your DAW with a midi keyboard or draw it in on the piano roll. It's all about quickly, getting your ideas from your mind and into the computer. Experiment and don't judge yourself.

Once you have your pattern recorded in you want to start thinking about the key of the melody. Find where you want the root note to be. To help you maybe choosing a basic sound at first is a good idea. Test it and listen to where it sounds good. Incidentally at this stage I would usually use a generic piano sound to test out melodies and chords. If it sounds good on there then it will sound good on any other preset. You can always keep moving the arrangement onto the piano to test out the intricacies.

With your root note set you can then start to move the different notes around in the scale. To help you stay within the key scale just draw the notes of the scale into the piano roll of your DAW and then mute them so that you have a visual representation of the key you are working in. Once you have a decent one bar loop melody, start to change it up across the following bars. You want to aim to get a decent four bar loop that has a strong identity throughout. It should be catchy and not overly complex. Listen to The Chainsmokers, Calvin Harris and Dr Dre they all use pretty basic melodies but they are highly effective.

With your melody settled you can now throw down some chords. Record these in if you like or use your music theory knowledge to draw them in. The chords will set the tone and feeling of your loop. Remember to stay in the key of the song. The best way to start with chords is to think about the chord progression in your mind first. What is the rhythm? What is the emotion? You could play the chords in with a midi keyboard or draw them in. I suggest you start with the root notes of the chords. You can then layer some notes over the top to create the chords. This does not necessarily have to be the root note of the key scale. It's all about what you like and what emotions you are trying to convey. Often i like my chords and basslines to be a seventh or fifth below my melody. This creates a really harmonious sound with lots of space and intelligence. For more dancefloor stuff the melodies and chords stay quite basic throughout which allows the song to be more sonically powerful as there is less frequency movement. When you are done, make sure everything is locked in and quantized to the grid.

Bassline

To add to your melody and chords, let's create a bass. Think of how you want your bassline to play and sound. Then either record or draw it in. In most cases your bassline will use the root notes of your chord progression set an octave lower. You could then change up the rhythm a little bit to keep it exciting. Maybe you have an offbeat bass that moves around the kick or maybe your bass is long and slow to come in. Use your imagination and create your vision. The bassline should support the loop and not take away from it.

MIDI and Presets

One of the most difficult things guys for anybody in the creative world is creating a melody and chords. If you show up to the studio and you don't have these ready then your going to struggle. A great and easy way to start a song is with MIDI melodies and chords. Maybe it doesn't feel like the song is yours, however as producers we want to be efficient and instead of wasting hours trying to make a melody, could just use some MIDI. The important thing here is that you have something to start with. MIDI can easily be changed later on and it can then become something more original to you. To find MIDI files just do a quick Google search. You could even find the MIDI of your favorite songs and then try to change or borrow a few ideas.

Other times you might not have any idea or MIDI. In this case what a lot of music producers do is fire up one a VSTI and start scrolling through some presets. Finally you find that one sound and you're like wow I know what to do with this. Boom, the song is done in your head and it's time to get action. To do this you don't need a lot of sound banks or presets, most VSTI's come with great stock plug ins that are equally as good. So go preset scroll guys and hopefully you find a great sound that inspires you to make some music

Beats

Next up you will want to add some drums to support your musical arrangement. Creating good drums is all about choosing the best sounds. You can go in three different directions. Record a full drum set, use loops or create loops with single sampled drum hits. Recording a drum set is quite a complicated task and is only something you would consider if you were working more with live bands. For that purpose you would require a great drummer, awesome microphones and utilization of professional recording techniques. There really are a lot of intricate parts to the process and if you compromise one then the final sound can be really bad.

If your starting out or even at a professional level it is better to use samples. Check out www.splice.com, it is a game changer. For a small subscription paid monthly you get access to a library full of quality samples and presets that you can find listed in various, tags, key and bpm. The service is based on credits so for every download you use a credit and the number of credits you have depends on your payment plan. In addition you can also rent to own some of the leading VST and VSTI's. It really is next level stuff to finding the perfect sounds for your productions. This is great for creating loops or making loops from single, sample drum hits. When it comes to finding the right loop of course you need to have the idea right and then search for the appropriate bpm and feel.

If you decide to start creating beats with individual hits then it will be a highly effective way to create really unique drums that specifically meet the requirements of your songs. The most important part of the process comes in the sample selection. It is like baking a cake, find the right ingredients and you have a great product. Use the rotten ones and it will be bad. What I suggest you do is to start sourcing a few different hits each time and then compare them to find the best. To make it easier you can just load them into your sampler of choice, draw in a pattern in midi and then switch between the different sounds. Decisions should be based on achieving the right pitch, envelope and timbre to gel with your other instruments. Later you can add effects and mixing to gel them together even more.

The main drum elements to build around are usually a kick and snare. The first thing I like to start with is finding a really good kick. It is the foundation of most club music and it really moves you in the club or at a festival. If you select the wrong kick you're kind of already screwed from the start, it would be really hard for you to get anywhere good. If you do find good kick samples you can reuse them on on your tracks. Don't be one of these people that always wants to use something new for the kick, go for the ones where you know that they will work well. The kick should always be in the key of the song, in most cases this would be the root note. Most samples will tell you what the key is but you can also check it out with the stock plugins available in your DAW.

Once you have found a good kick and snare sound you can program in the right pattern for them. Usually that would be quite a simple one and with a drum roll every sixteen bars. Then you can start to fill in the blanks of the frequency spectrum with other drum hits or loops. However this all depends on the music your making, the less melodic it is the more drum elements you usually have so if your melodies are not that interesting and exciting you have to do other things instead. You can fill up the high and high mid frequency range with shakers and hi hats. Or you can also add in some drum breaks to fill up the spectrum nicely. I also like to add some background drum rolls and breaks just as some kind of ear candy. Keep bringing things in and testing them out but make sure they have a purpose and fit the music. It all depends on what kind of music and the vision for it you have.

Tempo

The tempo/ speed of your song is going to have a massive impact on it. You can experiment with different tempos whilst your song is in it's loop stage. Don't get stuck in the box, try out a bunch of different variations. What works really well is to produce a number of variations of your musical elements and melodies before you start to arrange it. You could try it at a really slow tempo with different patterns for your melodies and drums. Or you could go more fast with the tempo and arrange things into a more dance floor structure. Just experiment and go with what you like the most.

To give you some ideas of common tempo's take a look at the following.
Trap and Future Bass - usually around 150 to 155 bpm
Big Room and Progressive EDM - usually around 128 to 130 bpm
Hip Hop - usually around 95 to 105 bpm or 140 to 150 bpm
Tropical House - usually around 100 to 105 bpm
Pop - a lot of pop music is around 100 bpm but there are lot's of variations that incorporate the elements and tempos of other genres such as EDM and Trap.

Arrangement

At this stage you should have a good melody, chord progression, bassline and drums. This will serve as the main part of your song, it's the hook or chorus. Many producers often find it a struggle to turn their loop's into a full song. Don't worry if this happens because you're absolutely not alone, almost all musicians and producers struggle with this. Actually there's loads of practical things you can do to help turn this loop into a song. The first one is all about arranging your song so that it can have structure variety and interest. The second one is about jamming along with the song whether you're by yourself or with friends. You can add creative musical parts as you play along to your song adding things to keep it interesting. The third part is all about how to mix refine and organize your project as you go so that you stay motivated to work on it.

A song is a story that takes the listener on a journey from the start to the end with feelings and emotions. The first step that you can do to get a loop into more of a song format is to actually structure it like a song. There is no standard with this kind of thing but we can look at some of the most common ways to structure a song. Later when you are more experienced you can experiment with different structures. It all depends on what your vision for the song is. Is it aimed at the dancefloor, the radio or for at home listening? If you want to get great at producing tracks start analyzing more music. Pay attention to the arrangements, how do they progress and how do they capture and keep the listeners attention? Famous commercial music producers who are making these smash hits are smart and their songs are constructed so well. I encourage you take an in depth look at some of their music and even spend some of your time trying to reproduce famous songs. Import the whole song and figure out the key, structure, instruments and everything else. If you do that reguraly I guarantee you're going to learn some stuff and you can go apply it to whatever else you want to do.

Commercial Music Arrangements

Culturally our ears have been pre-programmed to expect certain things at certain times in music. In commercial music there are four main sections to most songs. A pre chorus, chorus, bridge and verse. A chorus is the main hook of the song and is obviously where you want someone to go to iTunes and click buy. Verses are usually the chill parts of the songs. That's where you're going to tell your story and sort of setup what's to come.The main rule with commercial music is every eight bars you throw something new in because ideally you want to build your songs and carry the listener on a journey.

To start you can begin with a verse or some kind of intro. Normally after a verse we know a choruses is on its way even if it's a pre-chorus we know we're building to a chorus and the listener will expect them to happen at certain times instinctually. After a chorus comes another verse or bridge and if something weird happens it throws people off. By the end of the first chorus you want people to know the song already. When the second chorus comes in you want the listener to already be hooked in and sing it without hesitation so don't change anything, keep the same arrangement. After chorus two you can go to a bridge. At this point the song is as big as it has ever been. It's the most energy that's ever been in the song. A bridge usually happens once in a song and it's sort of your time to get creative like if you want to do some crazy stuff musically there's your spot to do it. Often it is exciting and builds a lot of tension. After that you're usually going to go into another chorus or sometimes depending on the song you can go into another verse but after that it's pretty much like we've hit the peak of the song and we're driving out the chorus. Right then after the bridge we bring things down it's sort of like the calm before the storm the calm before the end of the tune where we just really want to drive it out with the outro which is usually another chorus with some added layers such as more vocals or instruments.

Watch your song lengths overall time. Try to keep it under four minutes, maybe you want to write epic six minute long songs. If your song is seven minutes long it's not going to cut it and you've got to chop it down. Your really not going to see much of anything past five minutes in length.

EDM Music Arrangement

In EDM the structure of a song is a lot more simple because the majority of them are made for the dancefloor and need to be easy for a DJ to mix. The songs are meant to make people dance and are usually three to four minutes long with an intro and outro for DJ to mix in and out of the track and lots of build ups and drops. Typically you will have an intro, build up, drop, break down, drop and then outro. Each section is usually changing every sixteen bars.

The first section would be an intro of sixteen to thirty two bars. A trick I use is to construct this kind of music is to take the main drop part and mute different parts to see what could work as the intro. Or you can take the melody and remove a few notes. Once you figure that out you definitely have made good progress. The intro part should slowly build up as more elements are introduced. This will then go into some kind of breakdown. Usually the drums will stop here and it will be more atmospheric with vocals or some melodies progressing over sixteen to thirty two bars. This will then go into a build up across sixteen bars. This part is really important and you want it to bridge your breakdown into the drop. I suggest you spend awhile on this and test how it sounds transitioning into the drop. You can make some really epic build ups that will make your music highly original and memorable.

Reaching the drop is like your main chorus. It's where your main melody is played along with drums and the full power of your arrangement. This usually last about thirty two bars with some kind of variation in the middle and then a little bit of a different arrangement on the next sixteen bars. Often that is just the addition of a few extra drums, hi hats or extra notes and or variations of the melody. Then the song would breakdown to another atmospheric part that is similar to the first part. A lot of EDM music will use this section to have some kind of synth and chords arrangement for sixteen to thirty two bars here. It's kind of like a bridge where you can show of your musical skills or some really cool sound design. Keep it relevant to the key of the song and perhaps use some new sounds. You can then go back into the build up and another drop. The drop is usually the same as the first one or if your feeling experimental you could try something a little different. Hardwell does this a lot on his second drops as does Dillinja. Listen out for both of them. Finally to finish your EDM song would be the outro which is like the book end and build down of the song. You could then end it with an impact hit, effects or fade out. It's all up to you.

Sound Design

When you have a good vibe going on with your song and the construction is tight the next part is sound design. This is often what takes the longest. Making a unique interesting sound is quite hard especially for synth sounds and is where you can spend a lot of time. This is the main reason why I advise you to separate the sound design from the arrangement part. Of course before you arrange you should have some kind of sound design going on. You can use some basic sounds and presets first off. Then get the arrangement and song idea down fast because sound design can take a long time and you might lose the vibe of the song.

The main reason for sound design being important is because the majority of instrument sounds aren't strong enough on their own. They need more support in order to sound bigger and cut through. Layering and sound design will help to achieve that. The first thing you want to do in this process is decide on that one main sound. Then you can start to add on other layers of sound. The first mistake that a lot of people make is to layer sounds that sound very similar to each other. The perfect example of that is layering supersaws. Yes it's going to sound bigger but you can get the same effect if you were to just compress and put the volume up. So in the case of layering there would be no need to put another synth in the mix.

Layering is all about filling in the areas that are missing in a sound. To help you with decisions, it's a good idea to find a song to reference to. Identify what is missing in your sound versus the reference song. If it's more high end then find a nice bright synth. Or if it lacks a real live feel, then add live instruments and so on. Be objective and purposeful in your decisions.

Another thing to consider is that you make sure you are getting a good balance of mono and stereo. For example, when it comes to layering lead sounds one of your layers should be in mono and then one can take care of the stereo field. This will ensure that the overall sound is mono compatible and it won't get lost in the mix on some mono sound systems.

Finally you want to mix all of your layers into one channel. The benefit of doing that is that now we can compress the individual sounds together. A lot of the time when you layer leads together they will have different dynamic levels. If we glue and compress them together so that they have the same dynamic level it is going to sound more unified. In addition if you want the leads to sound very similar to each other then you can have the same effects on them which would be added to the bus channel. Reverb is great to bring life to the layered sound. There are two ways you can add your reverb. The first way is to add the reverb to a new bus and send the lead signal there or you can just add it to the bus channel. The first option usually creates a better result with a cleaner reverb. To the layered sound I also recommend to add some saturation to gel it together more.

Keep working on your sound design. You can create some really cool sounds but don't get stuck on the details for too long. Focus on finding the right sounds and creating a composite mix of how you imagine it to be. Finally make sure you get it right before you start mixing the song. These are two separate processes and going backwards and forwards between them will waste time and kill the vibe.

Automation

Automation allows us to take any sound and get it to change over time. This will keep the structure and sound design of your songs interesting. You want to keep your listeners locked in. For example you could take a bassline and instead of it coming in really punchy at the beginning you could open up the controls and set it to come in really light. As the intro is happening you could automate this filter to go up or down, whatever you want. Or you could make a sound disappear gradually with the reverb coming up. Most settings on channels, plug ins and instruments can be automated. It is just a case of you simply finding on a parameter and then automating it as you desire. This can be achieved by either recording the movements in or drawing them in by hand onto the particular automation lane.

Reference

Using a reference is a really simple but commonly overlooked method of improving your mixes and productions. You can select a song or a group of songs that you really like for several reasons, including the mixing the mastering, the composition, the arrangement, the sound design or any other factors. It doesn't have to be the most popular music in the world. Simply good music that you aspire towards being able to create or being able to mix in a similar manner. The idea behind this technique is that you can analyze these reference tracks and compare them with the songs you're working on to determine what is lacking or excessive.

A lot of the time when we hear good mixes we're not necessarily in our studio. We might be in the car might or in the gym, who knows where you might be listening. Essentially you need to know what that mix actually sounds like if you were in your studio. Your ears become used to the music you're listening to, so if you're listening to something with a bad mix then your ears have kind of adjusted to the imbalances. If you then listen to a professionally finished mix or one of these reference tracks that you really like it sort of resets what the balance should sound like. You'll immediately be able to hear what you need to change in your song. All of these problems will become really apparent to you. Overall this saves you time if you have something to work towards. If you have something to work towards it's going to save you time because you know what you're aiming towards. Then you can make decisions a lot easier to try and fit your track into that sort of mold. With that being said you're not trying to copy the track. It doesn't matter if your kick drum doesn't sound the same, or your bass doesn't sound the same, or you're using a different snare. That's all completely fine, it's more about the general picture.

Hey, I hope you're enjoying this book….if so please share your feedback with a good review.

Recording

If you want to add in some live instruments or vocals to your songs then it's a great way to make them more original and interesting. Or maybe you are a great guitar player or singer. This will set you miles apart from the majority of producers who are just making music on their laptops. You should always strive to expand on your ideas and more musical minds can create a better song. If you decide to record some instruments or vocals then here are eight tips to help you out.

Recording Tip One

Don't rely on fixing it in the mix. Simply taking the time to get it right in the performance stage will produce much better results. How you play greatly affects your sound. Don't expect to be good right away, practice really does make perfect and there's no magical plug-in or program to make you good. If you want a lot of energy on your recording then you have to record it with a lot of energy. If you want to record quiet then make sure there isn't too much noise or background sound. These kind of performance dynamics can't be achieved with mixing. Never make compromises in the performance stage believing that you can fix it in the mix. It is pretty much impossible to turn a bad recording into a good one. Nine times out of ten its better to go back and record it again.

Recording Tip Two

Use the best microphones, cables and audio interface that you can. Buy the best that you can afford and don't compromise on any of them. Even if you have an expensive interface that won't solve having poor quality microphones and vice versa. Microphone, audio interface and cable choice will greatly affect your sound and it will ultimately make your recordings much better or much worse. Have an idea of what you want. Are you going to do just vocals? Or are you going to be recording an entire drum set? Or are you primarily going to be a guitar player that records the songs at home? Those are very important questions that you need to ask yourself because that will be crucial in figuring out which interface and microphone to buy. These are all equally important parts of the signal. If you cheap out on one then it defeats the point of having one part that is really good.

Recording Tip Three

Know your parts. If you're going to go into a studio and pay a lot of money to be there you should probably know your parts and not figure them out there. Don't waste your money and don't waste the audio engineers time. It will end up being a much better finished product if you are as prepared as possible. Spend the bulk of your time in pre-production. You should be spending significantly more hours preparing your recording than the actual recording itself. Session time is expensive and others people's time is valuable. Do not waste that time fixing something that could've been fixed beforehand.

First and foremost the band, singers or players should be well-rehearsed. The arrangement should be worked out and everyone should know what is expected of them. It's a good idea to record raw demos of your rehearsal. You can analyse them and pinpoint the things you need to work on. You can then also can share them with the producer or engineer so that they know how to prepare for your recording session. If you have a producer on board discuss with them your goals and your inspirations. This will make sure everyone is on the same page and it will help plan out a course of action.

There also a number of small decisions you need to make. Will your recording be done live or will it be multi track overdubbed? Will you be playing with a click? All of these decisions will influence how you prepare. Scheduling should also be done in this pre-production phase. Write up a plan budgeting time for each part of the recording process. Plan on delays and synthesize extra time for creative noodling. Everything will feel better when nobody is stressed out about a clock. This still applies if you are working at your home studio. Try to have as clear a vision as possible and be objective. That way you won't find yourself recording track after track. The more organized and prepared you are the more fun you will have and more fun often leads to good music.

Recording Tip Four

Keep it fresh. This means put new strings on your guitar, new drum heads on your drums. Keep a clean and tidy recording environment. Make sure your singer is not hungover or sick. Be tuned and ready.

Recording Tip Five

Record your vocals clean and isolated. Not everyone has the luxury of an isolation room for recording vocals but if possible try and get into an isolated spot. This could be a closet, a bedroom or just a really quiet small room. I highly recommend a closet with the clothes still in it because that just deadens everything. If you record in a big open room you might get some reverb sound. Also try to avoid being in noisy areas. Having the window open is a bad idea if you live in a city. It is a lot easier to add reverb and sounds than it is to take them out.

Recording Tip Six

Understand the tools. The more knowledge you have of the tools around you, the less of the barrier there is between your musical vision and the end product. Acknowledging music is power. Understanding how your software works, understanding how different microphones works and how it influences sound. Understanding plug-ins, understanding the role of everything in the studio. All these things are highly valuable tools.

Recording Tip Seven

Imagine a soundscape, a visual representation of the instruments playing. This helps organize and arrange the sounds. Ask what kind of feeling am I going for in this recording. For example, if it is a sense of intimacy than use less reverb. Maybe try to make it sound like in a small room. Or for example maybe you want really up front guitars, if so record them close up but be aware of the proximity effect (more on that later).

Recording Tip Eight

Be flexible and take criticism when you're recording. The whole point is for people to hear your music and you better be prepared for criticism because it's going to come whether you are ready for it or not. You should actively seek feedback from the outside. When we are making music we are way into our own heads to be thinking objectively. This outside ear doesn't necessary have to be a musician. After all the untrained ear is going to make up the majority of people who listen to your songs. Ask your family, friends or whoever is around.

How to Record Vocals

There are a lot of variables to recording good vocals. First and foremost you have to be a good singer or have access to one. Because if you're not a good singer then as we already discussed your not going to be able to turn a bad recording into a good one. Again your microphones, cables and audio interface will make a big difference in terms of the sound, so select the best. The room you record in will also massively influence your recording. You probably don't have a whole lot of control over that if you have a home studio. However you can control the distance of your singer from the microphone in addition to microphone placement and how hot you record into your DAW (gain staging). Those factors will make a huge difference in terms of the quality of your vocals.

Another thing that is great for vocals is a pop shield which can be attached to the shock mount. What this does is it kills all the bees, peas and all the natural plosives that are in vocal sounds. When you say those sounds air blasts off your face and overloads the microphone. You probably have heard that sound, it sounds really amateur so don't record any vocals for anything until you have a pop shield. The pop shield will also help force a good distance. Most people record their vocals too close to the microphone and that's a major problem. The singer is just belting away and giving this awesome performance and their mouth is literally an inch or two from the mic. The side effect of being too close is called the proximity effect. When you take a directional microphone such as a cardioid microphone that picks up sounds in one direction. The closer you get to that microphone the greater the base response will be. So if you've ever been using a microphone for singing or speaking then you will notice that if you get really close to it you start to sound a little like Darth Vader because there's that added bump in the bass response. It has no choice but to sound super muddy, there's just no other option. So you record it there and you listen in your headphones while you're recording. Maybe you think yeah this is big, thick and awesome. But later when you go back to mix it you realize there is a lot of unnecessary low end to it. This is pretty much impossible to make sound good. The solution is to just back the microphone away a little bit more. Ideally it should be eight inches to a foot away. What you can do is to take the pop shield and put it about four four five inches away from the microphone. That will be like a boundary which says you can't get any closer and so your vocalist won't get any closer.

The next thing to consider is gain staging and this is so critical. Most people are recording too loud. You really don't need to record things that loud. If you're recording at 24-bit which is what most people are, then you have plenty of headroom and the noise floor is not really an issue. Turn that preamp down, when you're singing or your vocalist is warming up keep your eye on the meter and look at how hot it's getting. Then adjust the volume, the actual gain on that box on your preamp so that you're not peeking anywhere close to the top. You don't want to clip, record so that the meter is around fifty percent of the way up. It will peak a little bit over fiftty percent on some of the loud parts but on average you want to keep it below fifty percent. When you record that low on the meters it looks really unmanly. You feel unmanly and it doesn't look cool to have it way down there. But what matters is, does it sound cool? Because it will sound better when you record it quietly. Not super, super quiet to the point where you can't do anything with it but just fifty percent of the way up is a great starting point. Now if it's not loud enough to you and if you can't hear it or your vocalist is saying turn me up then you don't turn them up on the preamp because you've already got a good level. You turn them up in their mix, it's really easy to set up your headphone sends for their mix and turn that up so they hear what they're hearing. Do not turn up the actual preamp or the audio interface because that's going to affect the actual signal so keep that where you need it.

In conclusion recording good vocals is all about setting the right distance from the microphone, good equipment, acoustics and gain staging. You can apply these principles to recording most instruments also.

Adding Effects and Mixing

Now your at the mixing stage where you can take your song to the next level. It's all about achieving a good balance here. You also need to be objective and productive, don't spend hours here. So many people lose a lot of time here that is completely unnecessary and they end up getting nowhere. If you're feeling overwhelmed by mixing then don't worry because below are fifteen tips to help you succeed.

Mixing Tip One

Before you mix anything make sure it is right at the source. I know you've already heard this but I really can't stress the importance of this enough. Think of it like building a house. If you use bad materials that are decaying and poor quality then no matter how good of a builder you are the end result won't be good. If your recording and mixing, make sure you've got good material. Spend the majority of your time during the recording and production stages. Mixing will be much easier if you put the majority of your efforts there.

Mixing Tip Two

Focus on setting a good volume balance at the start. The foundations of a great mix down come from achieving a good balance of volume at the start and it is paramount to do this properly. Spend the first part of your time on balancing the volume only. Make sure you achieve a great volume balance before you start adding any other plugins or do anything else. Otherwise you will be constantly redressing this during the mixing sessions. You will also need to use volume automation since it is hard to achieve the perfect balance during the whole song. Maybe in some areas the vocals are jumping out or maybe too quiet and automation can adjust that for a particular section.

Mixing Tip Three

Time is essential and mixing sessions should not waste any time. The more time you spend mixing the more difficult it becomes to stay objective. As time progresses you start to lose perspective of what the mix really is sounding like. In addition if your mixing at higher volumes you will also be succumbing to ear fatigue. Make sure you put in time that counts. Prepare your mix before you start. This will allow you to stay objective and be able to mix fast and productively.

Mixing Tip Four

Focus on the main parts. Don't get lost over EQ'ing or compressing some small detail or sound effect in the background. The majority of your mixing should be focused on the mix as a whole picture. Take the stuff that really matters, the vocals, the leads and the main parts. Your priority should be making the stuff that is the listeners focus sound the best. The other elements will follow suit and fit with them.

Mixing Tip Five

Set a loop around the loudest part of your song. When you're doing that preliminary volume balancing it should always be at the chorus or the climax of the song. Mix from this loop because if you use a verse or intro then you can't really build up from that. For example if you had this huge intro then it doesn't leave much room to go from that. The majority of your mixing, adding effects and things should be done at the loudest part. You can always go back to the other sections and add in some volume automation to adjust them if you need to. Your song should really explode into the loudest part with impact.

Mixing Tip Six

Always stay within the big picture. You might think that it is making a difference starting out with EQ,ing and compressing a kick. After all it is one of the most important elements and so you decide to focus loads of time there and then start bringing in other elements. But what you will find is that when you get near the end of the mix, the kick suddenly doesn't work as well. This is because you didn't have it mixed in the context of the mix. Maybe it's conflicting with the frequencies of similar instruments such as the bass synthesizer or maybe it's causing interferences with something similar in the mix. The only way you can really know if you mix it in context with the rest of the mix.

What I strongly suggest is that you begin the mix with the focus on the big picture. Take big broad sweeps and begin with processes like mix buss processing, group processing and the volume balancing. Later on you can zone in on those more intricate details of the mix. Avoid using the solo function of a channel if you can because it takes your sounds out of the context of the mix and then you're probably making the wrong decisions and wasting time. Afterall the listeners won't be listening to anything in solo so try not to use that function, you need to always be in context. If you do struggle with making changes without soloing a channel you can just turn that channel up and make your changes. You will still be in the context of the mix and then you can just drop it back down to where it was. Practice it and develop your hearing.

Mixing Tip Seven

Make sure there is intent behind all of the moves you make. Never do something just because everyone does it or even just for the sake of it. So many producers easily fall into this trap. For example you don't need to apply compression every time, anyway most sounds are already heavily processed. First decide on your intention before taking action. Try to listen with intent and think before you act. Let's say the kick drum is not clear enough, it doesn't stand out and so you apply EQ to emphasize that so that it's really cutting through the mix. But if the kick is already clear in the mix then it doesn't need anymore. Simply leave it as it is. Before making any decision you have to first ask yourself, what am I trying to achieve?

Don't assume you need EQ or compression or effects on every track. The tendency is to slap a plug in on every single track and start fixing or enhancing with the assumption being that every track could be a little bit better with it. Be objective and ask yourself does this track really need any help. If it doesn't and if it sounds good already, then don't put anything on it. The fewer plug is you use the more natural your mix will sound.

Mixing Tip Eight

Analyze your moves. Any time you apply a plugin or change something in the mix, match the volume so that it's the same volume coming out as going in. To be sure you can activate the bypass button to check for volume. Bring it back in with volume and once you've got the same volume turn that bypass button on and off a few times. Does it sound better? Sometimes you might fool yourself so a good thing to do is click it then shut your eyes and turn it on and off many times until you can't remember if it's bypass or engaged. Then you can decide on if it sounds better because then you're really using your ears.

Mixing Tip Nine

Reference your mix against professional songs. This is the process of using a professionally mixed song to check against your mix so you can hear where you're going wrong what you might need to do. Don't use one, try three or four because then you get a better range of reference material. Use a few in a similar genre and in the same key because the bass will change in volume when key changes. It could even be songs that you've mixed in the past that you really like or they could be from up-and-coming artists and mixing engineers. It's just anything that really inspires you and the mixing that you really enjoy.

So if you download the song and you pull it into your DAW you can just put it on its own track and compare it to your song. Pay close attention to specific of the mix against your mix. Low pass and listen to the low end. Does your mix have too many low frequencies or are there not enough? Analyze the top end, is there too much or not enough? How loud should the drums be? How loud is the vocal? Am i using too much reverb?

A lot of people will compare and find the finished track will be a lot louder because it's mastered. This can be really demotivating to compare your rough mix to a completely finished and professional product. So you need to start by level matching and just taking the volume down until it matches the rough volume of your track. Get used to the overall balance, mute it and then unmute your song and take a listen to it and just try to listen for overall differences. Use your ears you'll be able to hear pretty big differences and start honing in on problems in your own mix. But if you're not quite trusting your ears there's a few tools that you can use to help you out. The tonal balance tool from iZotope is pretty handy and this sort of breaks down the frequency spectrum into bands and shows you the distribution of frequencies, much like a spectrum analyzer. It can show you whether you have too much bass or too much high end compared to the references. Or you can listen to the reference track through that and see sort of what their curve looks like and then compare it to the curve or spectrum of your own song. You can see whether there's any peaks or troughs that don't really add up to see whether there's anything missing. As usual it's always best to trust your ears but sometimes having these extra visual tools can help you when mixing. But remember that it really does come down to your ears so just because a tool says that you're in the right tonal balance it doesn't necessarily mean it's right for your song. If you're not using references already then start doing this right away because it will massively improve your mixes.

Mixing Tip Ten

Most of your mixing should be done in mono. This will help you to create separation between sounds by using simple volume balancing, equalization and volume automation. Working in mono will push you to really get the best results between sounds. For example you must make sure there is nothing sticking through or clashing with each other. There should be clear separation and this has to be done primarily with setting volume and EQ. Once your near the final stages of the mix that's where it's okay to start panning and applying stereo effects. Then it will open out the mix because it will already sound very clear and separate. Stereo effects and panning will then make it even better. Most DAW's come with a mono feature or plug-in that you can apply to the master output and turn it off and on to go from stereo to mono.

Mixing Tip Eleven

Listen to your mix on various sets of speakers, sound systems and headphones. During the mixing process, this is an easy way to refresh your ears and perspective whilst checking how your mix translates across different systems. You can test it out on your pocket headphones, mixing headphones, your monitors, computer speakers, club PA, car stereo and anything else you have access to. It will sound different on each and your aim should be to strike a nice balance between all of those. Maybe that means some compromises on one system but for the better of them all. Testing it on the different systems and then going back to the mix to make adjustments will give you a well balanced mix. In addition it will also to reset your ears and give you a fresh perspective on the mix. Incidentally to gain more perspective and be consistent it's really important to take regular breaks, maybe every hour or so.

Mixing Tip Twelve

Mix at low levels. Many people mix way too loud and that is bad for your hearing and also decisions. When we turn things up too loud it often gives us an incorrect perception of frequencies. Ideally you should be mixing around the average level of conversations. If someone at the other side of the room can hear you speak when your mixing then your speakers are set at a good level. Or if you can clearly hear yourself speak, again the speakers are probably set at a good level. Going louder than that would be too much. However for example, sometimes you might want to go loud so you can really hear the low frequencies or sometimes you might want to turn it down so you can focus more on the vocals. In those cases you can use the volume knob as a tool but in the majority of cases you should be at conversational level.

Mixing Tip Thirteen

Take breaks often. We've already talked about this a little, but make sure you take regular breaks. Every hour or so is a good idea. Those breaks will help to reduce ear fatigue and give you a fresh perspective on the mix. Overall it will help you to maintain objectivity. On a macro level if your mixing day in day out you should try to take off a day every week or over longer periods maybe a week or more. Mixing can be very subjective and you can get buried in it. Sometimes you just need to step back and see what your doing.

Mixing Tip Fourteen

Never underestimate the power of volume automation. You can never achieve the perfect balance without using some volume automation. Each section of a song is different and the instruments will behave differently. For example at some sections the vocals become too quiet or there is a solo guitar section that you want to turn up in the chorus to increase the impact. Volume automation is a really powerful technique in this regard. It is extremely likely that the song will require some volume automation to maintain a decent balance during the whole of the song. But don't worry you don't you have to go and automate every channel, remember to be purposeful and listen to what is going on through the different song sections. Listen for things that suddenly start sticking out or that become too low. Volume automation is easy and can be done at the end in a few minutes.

Mixing Tip Fifteen

You don't need expensive plugins and you don't need to buy any extra plugins to achieve a great mix. Almost every DAW comes with good stock plugins and they keep on improving. Take responsibility and stop blaming your plugins if your not happy with your mixes. You can upgrade and start thinking about premium plugins when your mixes are sounding awesome using only stock plugins. Then it will just be about getting that final extra bit of quality with some new plugins. Try and keep it to a minimum, be minimalistic about plugins and have a go-to plug in for for every type of process. Have a go to EQ, a go to compressor, etc. You don't need to spend a fortune either. There are really good quality, affordable plugins out there, just take a look at the previous chapters.

Mixing Tip Sixteen

Be careful when using presets on your plug ins, they might seem magical and easy. For example, let's say you are working on the EQ of a male vocal and you load up a preset that says male vocal EQ. Why not, it makes total sense? However, what this does is it applies a specific EQ curve that the plug-in developers have decided is a good EQ curve for a male vocal. The problem with that is they have no idea what your vocal sounds like. In fact every preset would run into similar issues. They also have no idea of how it correlates within the mix. Essentially what they are doing is making suggestions of typical boosts and cuts on a male vocal. This makes sense in one regard because as you mix more you will stumble across some patterns and some go to starting points. But every vocal is different and this also applies to any other sound. Use them as a starting point but make sure they do what you want.

In addition, don't rely on visual references. If you find yourself making changes because you'd like to see a certain bump there or a certain cut there then you might be making mistakes. There have been so many studies done which prove our hearing is actually impaired by visual stimuli. In fact there is more brain activity when our eyes are closed listening to a piece of music than when our eyes are open. So actually looking at the screen while you mix can be dangerous. Use the bypass button, close your eyes and turn it on and off, on and off and see if it really is helping.

Now, lets take a look at some of the main tools we can use in mixing.

Compression

Compression is a tool that we use all the time in mixing. It controls volume and turns things down when they get too loud whilst turning up the quiet parts. Essentially it reduces the dynamic range of a sound. For example if someone talks loudly and quietly, a compressor will bring the levels closer to the same volume which makes it easier to hear.

Every compressor can be a little bit different but generally they will have the following components. Threshold, this determines when compression starts happening. If you pull the threshold down more compression happens and you can see that by the meter which will be showing the gain reduction. It will be telling you by how many decibels the compressor is turning the signal down. To set it just pull it down until some compression starts happening. On some compressors there is a knee control which sets the angle of compression. You can make it smooth for a gradual turning on of the compressor or more sharp for instant compression. Once the signal crosses the threshold the question is how much is it going to turn it down. Is it going to turn it down a little bit or a lot a bit? The parameter that determines is the ratio. The more we turn this up the more the signal gets compressed. Generally you should stick in the 2 to 1 and 4 to 1 ratio range and then occasionally go up higher if you need to have more aggressive compression.

Next up are gain controls. After the signal is compressed we need to use make up gain to get the volume back to where it was before compression so that we're hearing it at roughly the same volume. This allows us to hear really what's happening. If all we're hearing is volume difference we will think the louder one always sounds better. The whole reason we use compression and the only way to hear that is to make sure we've done some level matching before and after. Some compressors feature an input meter and also output meter which allows you to visually match things up. In addition some compressors have an auto gain button that will do that for you. sometimes they work well and sometimes they don't. In most cases it's more accurate and preferable to manually adjust.

The final two knobs that we need to pay attention to are attack and release. This has to do with how quickly the compressor turns the signal down once it crosses the threshold. Does it turn it down immediately or does it let some of the signal through and then turn it down? What determines that is the attack setting. This is one of the most important settings you can use when compressing. If you go really fast on the attack then it's going to clamp down on that signal really fast and it won't let much of a transient through. Sometimes that's exactly what you want and sometimes it's not. Personally I like to leave some attack time in there so that that punch can come through. Fast attack times can work well on things like vocals but I prefer slower attack times, usually on things like a drum buss or a snare drum by itself can be really cool with a fast attack.

If attack has to do with how quickly the compressor clamps down then release has to do with how quickly the compressor let's go of the sound. The faster we release the more we will hear the stuff that happens after. The longer we make the release the more the compressor will hold down on that signal and it will end up being kind of a quieter tone because we're not letting a lot of the in-between sounds come through. A lot of compressors will have an auto/adaptive button to set the release according to the signal. Again you can experiment manually versus auto.

Multi Band Compression

Multi brand compression is exactly the same as standard compression but with the ability to compress frequencies in four different frequency bands. Essentially it gives you four compressors for every band. They are low (about 0 to 150

Hertz), low mid (about 500 to 5 kilohertz) high mid (about 5 up to 15 KHZ and then high (about 15 up to 20 KHZ). Every multiband compressor r allows you to change these points and can compress every frequency range with a different setting. You can use multi-bang compression for example to just compress the low-end of a mix or maybe to squeeze the mid-range of a drum loop. It is a really helpful tool for shaping sounds and giving them a nice compressed, together sound without over compressing the whole frequency spectrum. Sometimes the low end might be fine and you just want to tame the high end a little bit.

Equalization (EQ)

EQ is an essential tool in mixing your projects. It is a very powerful way of processing sounds and making them fit in the mix. Essentially you can use it to either cut or boost a sound at a certain frequency range. It can help remove or reduce unwanted or resonant frequencies. Or it can turn up the ones that you want. It can be used to help clear up your mix by preventing different sounds from clashing in the same frequency band. When used in conjunction with compression it is a very powerful way of processing your sounds to your liking.

Every single sound that you hear is made up of frequencies. Different types of sounds and instruments tend to live in certain regions on the frequency spectrum. For example drum sounds such as high hats or claps reside in the treble and high mid regions. Leads, pads, vocals, guitars and stuff like that tend to reside in the mid to high mid regions. Whilst sounds like bass lines and kick drums tend to predominantly reside down in the sub and bass regions. Ultimately of course all these sounds can bleed over into the surrounding regions.

Equalizers have a number of bands that serve as control points along the frequency spectrum to let you manipulate sound. Each of these bands have properties associated with them. These properties are the frequency or where along the frequency spectrum you want the sound to be adjusted. Amount, which is set in decibels. A positive number means you're boosting and a negative number means you're cutting. The next property is shape or type. By default equaliser bands are usually set as a peaking type which looks like a bell curve type of shape. A bandwidths resonance or Q determines how wide or narrow the curve affecting the sound is. A much narrower band and will affect only a certain limited number of frequencies whilst a much wider band will affect a lot more surrounding frequencies. Narrow bands can be good for removing narrow resonant frequencies which sound bad. Wide bands can be used for a smooth boost in a region.

Another shape you can set is to use shelving. A low shelf would smoothly turn up or down low frequencies whilst a high self would do the same but to high frequencies. Then there are a high pass and low pass shape which basically states that any frequencies above or below where the band is set are allowed to pass. The difference from a high pass and a low shelf is that a low shelf goes down and then stays at a certain value whilst a high pass cuts off completely at a certain value.

Using an EQ is similar to how it's done in a compressor, it all depends on what you're trying to accomplish or what sound you're going for. Every single sound has its own special requirements. There's really no way that I or anyone else can tell you how to equalize every single sound so what I recommend you do is you get comfortable with EQ. Get good at using the tools and the techniques and before you know it EQ will become second nature to you.

De-esser

A de-esser is used to remove sibilant sounds from an audio recording. In most cases this comes from the really dominant S, F, T or Z sounds produced by vocals. These can really stick out and can be really sharp. The sharpness of these sounds is really determined by the microphone that you are using and the amount of compression that you apply to your recording. If you apply a lot of compression to your vocal recording these sounds can get a lot sharper. Also applying EQ in the high frequencies could make these sibilant sounds even more sharp.

The frequency of sibilant sounds is affected by the vocalist. Most de-esser plug-ins will let you choose between male or female settings and they even let you choose a frequency band. Essentially what it will do is it to reduce the sibealence by applying compression to that frequency group. In essence it is like a multi-band compressor but on the high frequencies only. When adding it to the signal chain if we're going to use a compressor and a de-esser it's best to use the de-esser before the compressor because compression will make the sibilant sounds even sharper. If we put a de-esser behind our compressor it has to work a lot harder so the best thing is to put your de-esser before the compressor so we actually already try to smooth out these sounds before we actually compress a vocal.

Reverb and Delay

Have you ever sang in the shower and felt like you should be singing on stage in front of thousands of people? Well that is because the bathroom is full of reverberation. In fact this used to be a common way to record singers and certain instruments. Stick them in a bathroom or any room with lots of reverberation and when you record them the microphone will pick up all the natural reverb of the room. These days we tend to record in dry rooms and apply a digital reverb or delay afterwards to create a sense of natural ambience and space.

Reverb is created when a sound is reflected from the surfaces or the objects around you. Walls, furniture and hard surfaces all cause a build-up of sound reflections to which then decay. Although you don't have to be in an actual room to create reverb effects you can also create artificial reverbs using plug ins. It is probably the most popular effect used in music but like with any effect if you use it too much you can end up spoiling a good sound. Reverb is mostly used to give a sense of realism to your sounds or you can go crazy and create wild and original sounds with huge depth. For example if your vocals were recorded in an isolation booth then they might sound a little bit dry. You can add reverb to liven them up. You can also use reverb to create space and push things back in the mix, normally with more reverb things will sound like they are further back. The best way to apply reverb is using a send and return. Simply you can put a reverb on a mix bus channel and then slowly send your signal to that channel. This will give you much more control and will sound a lot cleaner.

Many times either instead of or in combination with reverb we also use something called delay. Reverb and delay both create echo an effect. With delay you can create timed very specific echoes whereas with reverb the echoes build up in a more random way. As with reverb you can control the delay effect in many different ways. You can take the same single echo and make it happen many times or even make the delay echoes repeat at different times on the left and right stereo field. Sometimes we use delay instead of reverb but many times we use both.

Limiter

A limiter is something that is so commonly misunderstood and really horribly misused on in mixing, especially by beginners. In basic terms a limiter is just a really extreme compressor. Now a compressor as you may remember is something that we use to control the dynamic range or the difference in volume of a recording. The way you do that is you set a threshold and if the volume goes over that threshold it is reduced a little bit by a ratio that you set. This allows you to control the loud parts and then you apply makeup gain or a little bit of extra volume to get the quieter parts up to the same level. A limiter applies the same concept except when the volume hits the threshold it can't pass any further.

Limiters are usually used at the stage of mastering and that stage comes when you've mixed all the elements in your song. When using a limiter you've got two main aims and that's to raise the overall volume of the sound and secondly to stop loud peaks from coming through. The limiter has a threshold of zero dB and when the volume goes above that it's simply not allowed to pass above. You can apply a limiter so that you can turn the volume of your sound up without causing it to clip. This works great on squeezing together drums. Just be careful not to push it too hard and cause distortion, unless that is what you want.

Saturation

If you have been making music or mixing for a while then you've probably come across the term saturation. There are loads of different types of saturation and they all have their own special qualities and characteristics. Saturation types are often emulated on analog recording devices or mediums such as tape or preamps that are driven too loud. Unlike digital distortion or digital clipping where it hits zero and then it just starts cracking which sounds terrible, usually the way that audio breaks up in the analog domain sounds really nice and pleasing. All of these distortions and characteristics are all due to the imperfection of that recording medium but it just so happens to be that those imperfections actually sound really good to the human ear. Some people say it creates a warm sound. Experiment with lots of different types of saturation, it can really enhance your sound even if you're only using a small amount. Overall let your ears guide you and if you like the sound of it then that's the right one for you.

Chorus and Flange

The chorus effect is essentially duplicating a sound but slightly detuning it at the same time. In addition it also pans the sounds. Depending on your preference you can adjust all of these parameters to make the effect be more fast or slow. This is great way of adding warmth and depth to your sounds. It can turn plain narrow sounds into thick harmonies. Flange is similar but a little bit more extreme and is used more as an ear candy kind of effect. Be careful when applying it to bass instruments as it doesn't work too well in the lower frequencies.

Auto tune

You're probably already familiar with Auto-Tune, or rather, pitch correction. For most people "Auto-Tune" has become synonymous for all kinds vocal processing. But actually, the branded processor Auto-Tune can only do a specific set of things. The first hit single to use Auto-Tune was Cher's "Believe," and it used the most extreme setting, making it sound robotic in a way. That kind of sound had not been heard before, so within a year of the release of "Believe," Auto-Tune had been sold to every major studio in the world. The inventor said that Auto-Tune might be to music what Photoshop is to photography: everyone uses it, but not many are keen to admit it.

Basically, Auto-Tune takes the incoming signal, that is, the voice, and takes it to the closest note, making it in pitch. You can think of it sort of like a guitar where wherever you push on the neck, you'll get a real note because of the frets, but the voice without Auto-Tune is more like a violin, where you have to kind of slide around sometimes to get to the note you want. The pitch of a note is defined by its frequency, and this is measured in Hertz. The note A has a frequency of about 440 Hz while the closest note above it, A sharp, has a frequency of about 466. So if I would sing a note in between these two frequencies, Auto-Tune would try to correct it either to A sharp or to A. But changing the frequency is only part of what Auto-Tune does. Have you ever wondered why speeding up a song sounds like a chipmunk is singing? It's because you are increasing the frequency of the sound. But it also means you're shortening the note. So the cool thing that Auto-Tune does is that it changes the frequency and the length of the note.

There are a few positive things that modern vocal production has allowed for in music. First off, more precise vocal recordings. Secondly, it has allowed for faster work flows in the studio meaning that your favourite artists can make music way faster. So even though your favourite artist probably "cheats" a bit in the studio, try to remember that the tracks that you love by them might not have existed without this technology speeding up their workflow.

Mid Side

Mid/side processing has to do with the way phase works and sound is captured. Imagine that whatever comes from the center in other words mono means that it's being played at the same time on both speakers. Then there is everything else, whatever is played by the speaker's not at the same time that is going to be the difference. When you use Mid Side techniques instead of having left and right you have sum and difference. If for example increase the side part of the effect then your mix will be a lot wider. You could for example brighten up the side information and that will result in the top end being brighter but just in the stereo perception of the sound. Conversely you can decide for example to make the vocals louder just by pushing the mid of the side information. Or you may also decide to increase the low and just of whatever is mono in your mix.

There are many EQs available that have mid side capability, including stock plug-ins. Experiment with them and see what sounds best, find what works for you. Always make sure that you double check by pressing the mono button on your monitor so that you do not create any problems with the phase. You may choose to use mid/side compression, for example if you have backing vocals so you can decide to have a different behavior for compression on the sides or on the mono information that will change slightly the relationship of the backing vocals and the lead vocals within your mix. With all these techniques be very careful because you can change the sound quite dramatically. You should always bypass to check.

Analyzer

Spectrum analyzers give you a graphical representation of what's happening in the frequency range. In essence a spectrum analyzer allows us to see graphically what's happening within the frequency range. Many DAWs nowadays come with a spectral analysis built into every single individual track so you can use those. This is important because many of us being bedroom producers or having home studio setups don't have the greatest sounding rooms. Unless you have an acoustically treated studio space you know you're kind of at the mercy of you know your room.

What you might want to consider doing if you're going to start using a spectrum analyzer is to find a song that you think sounds amazing and use it as a reference. Look at the frequency curve of it compared to yours. If the frequency analysis doesn't look like the reference, no matter what you think it sounds like then your ears are deceiving you because the sound is bouncing around the room. You will be totally getting a distorted representation of what's going on.

An example of it's application could be to check the bump on the kick. Maybe you should have more of a bump and maybe turn up the kick or add some EQ at a specific frequency. Maybe you should raise the high hats or some of the upper register instruments. Use the analyzer as a visual guide and just really study the curve. Where are the bumps, where is it straight, where does it roll off? Use your eyes to help your ears and what you're going to find is as long as your curve matches their curve is that you've got a balanced mix.

In addition there are also analyzers for stereo width. Again you can check against a reference track to make sure your song is the right width. Typically you would do check across four frequency bands. Low, low mid, high mid and high. Most songs gradually widen from the low to the high. You can set those accordingly.

Side Chaining

Side chaining is a useful tool for allowing instruments at similar frequencies to fit together in the mix. The most common use of it is with a kick drum and bass line. Having a clear kick in dance music is really important and it can often get buried in the mix. There are two ways to use sidechaining. The first is with an LFO tool and the second using mix sends. If you use an LFO tool you would simply apply this to your bassline and set it's speed to fit with the pattern of the kick drum. The goal is that the lfo tool causes the bassline to drop in volume whenever the kick hits. You can adjust the envelope to suit this. I recommend you print your bassline and then import it back in as an audio file to ensure the ducking is correctly lined up.

The second way to apply sidechaining is a little bit more complicated. You need to use a compressor with the side chain facility available. Most of the big name DAW's will have a stock plug in featuring this. Next you need to insert the compressor onto the bassline channel. You would then select the input source to be whatever channel the kick is on. The signal from that will now be sent to the compressor causing to duck the volume of the bassline whenever the kick hits. This is great for other genres that don't use the standard 4/4 pattern of dance music. Since the lfo tool is more suited for that. You can then adjust the compressor attack and threshold to set how quickly and how much the compressor alters the bassline volume.

Be Minimal

A word of warning, you should be using as few plugins as possible. The reality is w we have access to so many great sounding plugins and we feel the urge to use so many. You can go crazy with effects and have as many versions of them inserted in your tracks as long as your computer can handle it. The temptation is to cover up our weak recordings with tons and tons of processing in hopes of turning it into something amazing. We shouldn't have to use so many plugins. Use as few plugins as possible. Technically speaking the more plugins you add the more processing and math your computer's having to do. More math means it's having to think harder and that affects the actual audio processing. In turn it doesn't keep the quality or the fidelity of the audio as pristine as it could be. The psychological benefit of using as few plugins as possible is it stops you in your tracks. It makes you ask yourself, what is this going to accomplish, what is the purpose of this plug-in? It forces you to have a reason for the mixing decisions you make which is so valuable. Work with great recordings and you will only need to do as little as possible. Don't harm your audio you don't over process it. Think strategically about what do you need to do and then you grab those tools and you use them.

Mastering

Mastering is the final process of enhancements and tweaks that we make to a song before it gets released or sent out. When you are happy with the mix and production it's time to get your song sounding big, fat, full and loud. You will want it to be just as good as all the other commercial stuff out there. There are many different ways to master and I'm just going to show you the way that I figured out over the years that's gotten me the most consistent results. Don't focus too much on the exact software or plugins, you can get great results with any program and any decent plugins. What I really want you to get is the principles. These can be explained in three stages, preparation, enhancement and checking.

When you are mastering remember that your ears get tired so you don't listen for hours and hours on end. Take regular breaks, every hour or son. In addition try and listen at a low volume for the majority of the time. At some times you might want to go loud in order to hear the bass and low frequencies. But don't get stuck there.

Preparation Stage

The first stage is to check through the track and make sure it is free from defects or sound artifacts. Make sure there's no noise and make sure there's no kind of clicks or pops. Before you even think about mastering it's really important to make sure it sounds the best it can be. Otherwise you will keep going back to the production and mixing stages. No matter how much you try and fix a bad recording or bad mix is still going to end up bad. Ideally you don't to go back to the mix phase or the recording phase but inevitably there might be things that you have to fix and at least you need to watch out for. Look out for obvious things like excess noise, especially in the beginnings and the ends or on the quiet parts things. Also different frequencies may be jumping out such as a certain bass note jumping out of the mix. Pay attention for those things because if possible it's better to go back to the mix fix.

Before you send out your final mix to be mastered, drop your input. When you are exporting your mix you want to aim for around minus 6 dB of headroom because you will need some room to play with. The headroom will allow you space to use your mastering tools. Next, set up you project. I recommend you import two or three reference tracks. These should be in the same key and have a sound that you would like your final master to be like. When you analyze your references against your song, the reference will look a lot fatter and bigger. That's what we are trying to get our song like. First what we're going to do is we're going to try and chop off any peaks and squash the whole thing down to get it to looking like the reference but more importantly sounding like it.

Enhancement Stage

The next stage is enhancement and this is just anything that makes the track sound better. It might be EQ tweaks, some exciters, bass boosts or dynamics processing, etc. If you are working on an album, it should fit in the context of a whole album. You want the tracks to flow from one to the next and so you don't want this really loud song next to a really quiet song.

Now in this phase there are a lot of things we can do to make it sound better. Maybe clean it up a bit or maybe just add a bit of something to it. For example maybe fatten it up a bit with low end boosters or add a bit of EQ on the top-end to brighten it. The first plugin I use would be just a standard EQ set up with a high-pass filter. All this is doing is just taking out all the frequencies below a certain point. You can set it really low at 40 Hertz and with a standard slope. This is just to clean up any potential low-end rumble. Since there's nothing down there that's that useful you can just cut it and allow more space in the mix. Low frequencies tend to take up the most space soe remove the ones that cannot be heard.

The next thing I would add is some valve or tube emulation. This will fatten up the mix a little bit and add some low-end meat. You can also add a tape emulator which will also add some bottom end and subtle saturation to the mix. Experiment with both, on some songs they will work and others maybe not. If your mix is still lacking low end you can use a great plug-in from Waves, called max base. What it does is to emulate and add frequencies in the low to low mid range. This is going to make the song sound fatter on smaller systems like iPod headphones, laptops and things like that. If you're doing music like hip-hop or trap it is an amazing plugin because often we lose fatness in a track. Because these saturation effects often take off some of the top end and makes it sound a little bit dull you will want to add a little bit of an EQ. Use this to add some sheen on the top end, but in a subtle way. Don't overdo it and make sure you check against your references. Also, always bypass to compare the dry origin. The EQ you use should be a very transparent.

Next you will want to add a little bit of compression to glue the track together. You should use it sparingly. You literally want like one or two decibels of gain reduction at the most. It should be just touching it to glue the track together a little bit more.

You can use a multiband compressor to actually solo each frequency because for example you may not want to compress the mid-range which is the most obvious part of the mix like where the vocals are. You don't want to compress that as much because it will result in sounding overly compressed. However you probably want to compress the low end and bass so that it sounds really fat without disappearing. Overall you want to set a threshold at the level that they are peaking at and then adjust the gain make-up to make it a lot clearer and just bring it all together.

The next thing I want to add is a stereo widener. I would suggest using a multi-band stereo widener so you that can set each band to be at different widths. Check against your reference tracks to hear how wide or narrow each band is. Should it be wider in the high, is it to narrow? Is the low end too wide? You can look at the reference screen and make adjustments accordingly. Most mixes will tend to be more narrow at the bottom and then widen towards the top. When you narrow bands be careful that it doesn't cause sounds to cancel eachother out. Always check before and after.

Next comes the clipping stage. what we're going to do here is chop off any peaks in order to get the mix more squashed and fat. However we don't want to distort the sound by pushing it too far because that will not sound good. We we want to use something that clips the signal but also sounds good and this is actually one of the secrets that the mastering professionals use to get songs really loud. They are actually driving them through these really expensive converters. Now you probably dont have really expensive converters. But you can use a decent saturation or clipper plug in to slowly saturate the track and chop the peaks off. Start playing the track and slowly push it until you hit the sweet spot. After that bring down the output to leave room for the limiter which we will add in the next phase.

The limiter is the last plug-in that you will use. This is the most essential plug in and what this does is to set the final output ceiling. The standard is to set it to minus 0.1 which means that it's not going to let any sounds go past minus 0.1. Zero is clipping so we are going just below that to avoid any clipping. Then as we drop the threshold of the limiter it'll start to limit and squeeze the sound more. We can also use a multiband limiter if we prefer so that it's actually limiting each band.

When it comes to setting the final volume it's a case of preference and reference. Compare to some of these other masters just to see where you are in terms of volume. You can use the metering function of the mixer to get an average level of the song you are referencing against. Remember to always bypass any effects so you can hear what they are doing and if they are working as you want. If your mix is sounding louder or quieter than your reference record then you're probably doing something wrong. Usually it has to do with the low end because it's easy to get a song loud and sort of like harsh signing but to get it loud and fat that is the challenge. So if you need to go, go back and adjust your signal chain until you get your master how you want it.

Checking Stages

The final step is to export the mix and test it on a whole bunch of different systems. Try it on a small radio, headphones, in the car on something with a subwoofer or in the club, wherever you can. The goal is so that you can hear what that sounds like on the different systems. However don't make final decisions based on one system but if you notice that say on like four different systems the bass is too high or it's sounding too thin on all the different systems then it probably will need those adjustments. If you can strike a great balance on all the systems then you have a winning mix.

Finally then comes the formatting and this just involves all the admin things like naming the tracks putting in some kind of codes in case you want the names to come up and the album cover to come up in some media players. It is also the final format stage that you're saving this whole thing to. Is it going to CD or is it going to MP3? For CD quality settings you will need to export at 44.1 kHZ with bit rate of 16 bit. For MP3 you will need to export at 320 kbps with a bit rate of 16 bit.

Hey, I hope you're enjoying this book….if so please share your feedback with a good review.

Conclusion / Finding Your Sound

Your sound isn't something you discover once and for all in fact it's something you develop. So if you're sitting down to produce or write just one song, instead of sitting around and trying to discover what that sound will be before you do anything you might want to just start with the rough idea of the song. How are you going to know what your sound is before you even start making music? It it just doesn't make sense, it's like having an author say I want to be an author and I want to know what my writing style is in my voice without ever writing anything. To be an author you have develop your own voice and write more books. The same is true for you as a musician and an artist, you have to record songs, write songs or release songs to develop your sound as an artist. Now imagine that over a course of an album. Imagine that over the course of a career as an artist. It is the long term process of making music and putting it out there that will develop your sound. Laying down a simple track or creating a drum loop won't develop your sound.

Think about your favorite bands or artists, they all have a distinct sound. When you're sitting down to write music and create music you should always be developing you sound. Everyone has to figure out their own unique sound. A common mistake people make here is that they can't sound like anybody else. That's kind of an arrogant position. There are very few people who are original and even those people aren't truly original because we have all been influenced by someone else. Your goal shouldn't be to sound totally unique and unlike anyone else because in doing that you start from a negative place of I don't want to sound like them. Come at it from a positive place which is who do I sound like or what do I want to sound like. The difference is huge because you can create and discover your sound when you're looking for what you want as opposed to saying this is what I'm not.

Let yourself intentionally be influenced by other artists. Look at artists or bands or records or specific songs that you want to listen to and intentionally try to be influenced by them. Now this is different than copying. For example, Daft Punk specifically wanted to recreate that seventies funk and soul sound on their last record and so they specifically listened to records from that era. They were heavily influenced intentionally because they wanted to kind of recreate that sound but what came out of that was a grammy award winning, completely original sounding record. Listen to a wide range of music, not just new music but older records too. You can develop and still sound fresh by borrowing ideas from decades ago. Let those influences come together and mash them into this incredible new sound. If you want to make great music you need to listen and obsess over great music all the time. Everybody is influenced, the only reason you know about music is because you've heard it. The only reason you know how to play guitar or piano or drums or whatever is because you've heard other people play. You are so influenced by other people, it's unavoidable and that is okay. The more you listen to great music the more ideas start popping in your mind and you actually can create faster.

The Power is in The People

Collaborate with other people, you can discover something new in yourself that you never would have done before. Having a network of other musicians, producers, engineers and people in the music space around you is probably the most important thing to developing your sound and becoming successful. Big opportunities often come from connecting with people, reaching out to people, jamming with people and taking calls with people. They don't necessarily have to be in your preferred genre. Ask any major producer or musician and they would say the same that their biggest opportunities came from connecting with other people and having a network.

Find music related events in your area and go to them.This could be events like on meetup.com or music expos or open mic nights anything that's music related that's happening in your area period go to it. If there's nothing in your area, go to another area where there is something happening. Check classified ads in your local paper or craigslist ads for engineers or musicians or mixers who are trying to get hired for certain gigs in your area and contact them. Not to hire them but just to tell them that you admire their work like. Say hey I just saw your ad on Craigslist or whatever you're super talented I love your work I'm not trying to hire you necessarily I'd love to just meet up for coffee man and just talk music with you and maybe we can encourage each other. Reach out to people you admire and offer anything you can think of for them and don't expect anything in return. Think about how you can add value to their life in any way. Generally people will give back and a lot of times what happens when you serve somebody like this they give to you without them realizing it. Your next big opportunity may not even come from the person you reached out to or the person you gave to but they will in turn pass your name along to somebody else.

No Excuses

Get out there and actually make some killer music. If you have good ideas, talent and a drive to make music then there are no more excuses to not make music. There used to be excuses. It used to be that equipment was expensive, the studios were hard-to-find but those excuses are out of the window. Most people will say I don't have the right equipment or the right room and a blah blah blah. Newsflash none of that matters, the gear you use does not matter that much. You can start with your affordable equipment and keep it and just use what you have and get better at it. Technical stuff will only get you so far even though that's what we think we need. But none of that will make any difference unless you have the correct mindset. That isn't just fluff, it's not motivational stuff but stuff that actually helps you achieve tangible results aka creating and releasing great sounding music.

Maybe what also holds you back is the common feeling that we never feel like we're good enough and there's always more to learn. You got to get over your fears and actually release some music. Realize you're not going to be amazing the first time you release something. Yes, there are some key things you do need to know to get really good sounding recordings with your gear but it's a lot easier than you think.

Maybe you never have the time. Your busy with a job, married and got kids. Music isn't going to be the most pressing thing in your life and so it gets pushed to the back. It gets pushed to the late nights, it gets pushed to the weekends, it gets pushed to next month which becomes next year and finally becomes never. But there are ways to better leverage your time so that you can do all the things you need to do and still have time for the things that you really want to do. You can always find time by cutting some things out that just aren't that important. If music is super important to you what you need to do is leverage something called the 80/20 rule. The 80/20 rule can help you not only get all the important and urgent stuff done faster but get all the important and non urgent things like your music making done in less time and with more quality. As a creative you need to learn this rule because it will help you get those things done that you want to get done and that means getting music made.

Stop Waiting

Stop waiting for inspiration to strike. It would be great if that were the case, if I'm sitting and eating a sandwich and all of a sudden I had this beautiful idea for a hit song. Most music is made by hard work. Most of the hit songs are written by songwriters that go to work every day and they write. They write hundreds and hundreds of songs, they record demos, they produce a lot of tracks and many never see the light of day. But that's how they get to the good stuff. You need to change your mindset and shift away from the wait for inspiration to strike mindset to create inspiration. But how do you force yourself to work on music making? By creating deadlines, deadlines that other people know about and hold you accountable to. Grab your calendar and decide what is it you want to do. Do you want to release an album? Do you want to release an EP? Do you want to mix for some new bands? Or do you just want to do a single? Whatever it is, decide a future. date on your calendar for when you're going to release it. Announce them publicly to at least one other person, ideally more than one person. You could go on social media and I say hey guys I'm going to release an EP on this date hold me accountable.

The moment you have a deadline things start to pick up and you feel that pressure. I've got to write some songs and get in studio. Even if you don't have time it creates time. Creating that forced deadline and then making it public will somehow magically help you find time even if it's pockets to get working. Somehow magically those pockets of time are more effective than they were if you had um limited open-ended time. This is because something called Parkinson's law, you can look it up it really does force you to get more done and get good work done.

Jump

Finally, get your music out there. You are no longer just a musician, producer, singer, songwriter or an artist, you are a brand. If you view yourself as just an artist then that means you're hoping that someone else will do everything for you. The things that used to be done for you by the industry which is to sign you and develop you as an artist get your stuff recorded, do all the marketing and promotion. This hasn't changed, if you want to grow and have people hear about you, you still have to market yourself. You still have to have do promotion, you still need to develop as an artist. All those things haven't gone away it's just that the burden has fallen on to you and you have to start thinking that you are the brand.

A brand is something that is sold, something that is marketed, something that people love and a brand is not a bad thing. Everybody is their own personal brand whether they believe it or not. If you want people to hear your music then you have to view what are all the duties that an entrepreneur or a business owner would do to get his or her product or service or brand out there. That will involve you doing a little bit of research and shifting your mindset from not being just a creative and a musician but to also being somewhat of a business owner. Incidentally that will involve learning about marketing, promotion, branding and all those things

Now related to you being a brand you got to view yourself as a content creator because we are in an age that loves to consume content. We love to scroll in our feeds and consume little bite-size content. It is a culture of boredom and a culture of getting lost in the black hole of more content. As an artist or musician you need to be a content creator. What that means for you is you don't just make music. Music is the hub of what you do but you don't just make albums and try to sell them or try to get them on the radio. You have to start viewing yourself as more than just I'm going to mix album or an EP or something. You are a content creator and your content happens to be music but it can also be other things. It could be video of you in your studio recording, it could be video of you songwriting, it could be an interview with you in the band, it could be live footage of you onstage at a show and so on. It could just be you talking to your fans about what you do on the weekends when you're not doing music or the inspiration for a song. There are a million things that you could do as an artist or band to create pieces of content short or long that would go alongside your other core content

The old rules involved just focusing on your music and the rest would come. Not today, you've got to be a brand and think about what it takes to be a brand and you have to be a content creator and create that engagement with your audience. Get your stuff out there, it doesn't have to be perfect. The old way was perfection, you had an artist or a band that was always presented perfectly. You'd be presented with your record which would sound amazing and be perfect and you'd be presented with a killer music video which would be perfect and amazing. That was the era that many of us grew up in.

Nowadays if you just want to release something once every two years and then nobody hears from you in between that time, well it just won't fly. Your audience will move on without you and they'll find someone else to to follow. You need to show up regularly. That could be every week, that could be every month, that could be every couple of months or it could be everyday if you've got the time. But how do you do that? You can't create polished amazing records or music videos that are full-blown productions every day or every week or even every month. Instead you need to embrace imperfection and start sharing stuff that's not finished. Don't spend forever on them just put it out there even if it's not perfect. Or don't release an album, instead just release singles once every month. Yeah you could spend ten more hours on it, but it might not be that much better and no one's gonna notice. Sorry to say, the moment you finish just it get it out there and then you can move onto the next project. Every time you move on to another project even if it's one song you will be approaching it with fresh ears, a fresh perspective and an increased awareness of what you can do better and what you did well last time.

Embrace the journey and enjoy it.

Music Production: The Advanced Guide On How to Produce for Music Producers

Tommy Swindali 2018

Copyright Notice

Disclaimer

Reasonable care has been taken to ensure that the information presented in this book is accurate. However, the reader should understand that the information provided does not constitute legal, medical or professional advice of any kind.

No Liability: this product is supplied "as is" and without warranties. All warranties, express or implied, are hereby disclaimed. Use of this product constitutes acceptance of the "No Liability" policy. If you do not agree with this policy, you are not permitted to use or distribute this product.

We shall not be liable for any losses or damages whatsoever (including, without limitation, consequential loss or damage) directly or indirectly arising from the use of this product.

Tommy Swindali 2018

Claim your FREE Audiobook Now

Music Production: Everything You Need To Know About Producing Music and Songwriting (Two Book Bundle)

Everything you need to know about making music in one place!

Grab your chance to own this two book audio bundle by Tommy Swindali.

Covering

everything you need to know about music production, as well as songwriting.

Including:

Music production: How to produce music, the easy-to-listen-to guide for music producers

Songwriting: Apply proven methods, ideas, and exercises to kickstart or upgrade your songwriting

Are You Ready To Start Earning REAL INCOME With Your Music?

https://www.subscribepage.com/musicbiz

ENROLL NOW! [Limited Spots Available]

Other Books by Tommy Swindali

In The Mix: Discover The Secrets to Becoming a Successful DJ

If you have ever dreamed of being a DJ with people dancing to your music and all whilst having the time of your life then this book will show you how. Find Out More

Music Production: Everything You Need To Know About Producing Music and Songwriting

Everything You Need To Know About Making Music In One Place! Grab your chance to own this comprehensive guide by Tommy Swindali. Covering everything you need to know about music production, as well as songwriting. Find Out More

Music Production: How to Produce Music, The Easy to Read Guide for Music Producers Introduction

You are about to discover proven steps and strategies from music producers on how to produce music, even if you have zero experience in recording and audio engineering. You will be able to learn everything you need to know in order to make your first single sound just the way you want it. Find Out More

Songwriting: Apply Proven Methods, Ideas and Exercises to Kickstart or Upgrade Your Songwriting

Have you ever listened to a song and thought "wow, if only I could write a song like that"? Well, you can now learn all the

secrets on how to write beautiful music with this guide to songwriting! Find Out More

In This Book You Will Discover

With all the music production advice out there, it can be very easy to get overwhelmed. You may get a vague idea of the general topic, but you're more likely to be confused and you definitely won't have any workable knowledge.

Well, the good news is this book changes that. Designed to take the complex world of music production, and explain it in simple terms. If you are a DIY musician, this is a must have for making your music sound professional. For the pros and semi-pros out there, this is a great book for understanding what good music production entails.

You can apply this knowledge to any genre of music. Your Music will sound balanced, clean, professionally mixed and you will be on your way to having a successful career in the Music Production Industry. The barrier to entry for making music is practically non-existent these days. That's why success can only come from you and not the equipment you use. While knowing how to use your tools is important, it's about the drive within that will **take you to the next level.**

Introduction
   Should You Study?

The Fundamentals of Music Production
   Music Theory
   Science of Sound
   Digital Sound

Build Your Dream Studio: Computer Music
   Computer
   Software
      Pro Tools
      Logic Pro X
      Ableton Live
      Fl Studio
      Reason
   Plug Ins and Virtual Synthesizers
      Waves
      Izoptope
      Fabfilter
      Valhalla Room
      Guitar Rig
      Melodyne
      Sugar Bytes Effectrix
   VSTIS
      Komplete
      Serum
      Sylenth
      Nexus
      Spire
      Omnisphere

Build Your Dream Studio: Hardware

- Audio Interface
- Headphones
    - Sony MDR 75006
    - Audio Technica ATHM70X
    - BeyerDynamic DT 1990 Pro
    - Bowers & Wilkins P9
    - Sennheiser HD 800 S
- Speakers
    - Mackie CR 3
- Midi Keyboard
- Microphone

Acoustic Treatment

- Absorption and Diffusion
- Bass Traps

Producing Music

- Melody and Chords
- Bassline
- MIDI and Presets
- Beats
- Tempo
- Arrangement
    - Commercial Music Arrangements
    - EDM Music Arrangement
- Sound Design
- Automation
- Reference

Recording

- Recording Tip One
- Recording Tip Two
- Recording Tip Three

Introduction

Maybe you are thinking about a career in music production or making some beats. But you see the mountain of knowledge you have to acquire in order to live out your dreams and it seems impossible to get to the level of your production superheroes. The reality is that what these superstar producers do is just like everybody else. They sit in front of their computer for many hours a day and a lot of the days they come up with nothing. If you're passionate about music like them and you're willing to stick at it then you will eventually produce some hot tracks. This book is here to help you acquire all of the required skills and knowledge.

So what exactly is a music producer? A music producer is to a musical recording as a director is to a movie. When it comes to making a movie there is a line drawn in other words the buck stops there at the director. Look at the director as the captain of the ship who controls and steers the ship working with everyone from the technical editors to the actors in order to achieve his or her overall vision of the movie. A music producer should be the exact same. They should control and have the technical expertise and skills to produce a hot track. Simply put a music producer provides the experience to create a polished work of art.

The first foundation of being a music producer is a knowledge of music theory and that has nothing to do with computers. Because of the super fast growth of computer tools such as vsts and virtual synthesizers people get caught up in the whole technical aspect of music when they really should focus on the songwriting aspect. Music theory, chords, melodies, harmonizing, voicing and all of that good stuff. You need to understand a little if you're going to make it. It is the ability to come up with musical arrangements that evoke certain emotions that will either make you want to jump up, party or sob and cry. I cannot emphasize enough how important music theory is, it is by far the most important skill set.

The next foundation is sound design because at the end of the day there are only a finite number of chord progressions that you can come up with. The difference is in the textures and the sounds that you use to convey these chord progressions and melodies. Beginners in sound design are what I'm going to call preset users. Many people will tell you that presets are no good. You're cheating if you're making music with presets and so on and so forth. The reality is that everybody started out with presets. Once you get more comfortable you can start to tweak presets which is the second category. You start out with presets and once you get a good idea going then you can start turning the knobs, add effects and modulate the sounds to make them more unique. At the end of the day most of your production heroes, the people who chart and play on the radio every day are probably either preset users or preset tweakers. Once you're comfortable tweaking presets then there's the third category which are sound designers. Look at some of the biggest names, these guys surely program some of their sounds but they also use presets and some of their own unique sounds are actually just presets that they tweaked a little bit differently.

Overall you have to know where you reside. Understanding your place will help you be comfortable with who you are, let you know what you're good at and then you can dive deeper. Later on you should consider learning the more technical aspects of music production such as mixing and mastering. If you're comfortable with sound design, then maybe you need to improve your songwriting skills and vice versa. If you look at the best producers out there they all have a good mixture of these two skill sets. If you look at the the Hollywood composing scene people like John Williams. Most of his scores use standard presets which are unaltered versions of orchestral instruments. On the other hand you have people like Hans Zimmer who compose fairly simple music but are so good at sound designing that they get most of the contracts on the biggest blockbusters. Then, if you look at hip-hop producers such as Mike Will Made It or or DJ Mustard they are preset users and their compositions are fairly simple. But the way that they put it all together and the particular presets that they pick make them sound very original. Finally, if you look at the EDM world you have very good sound designers such as Skrillex, Diplo and Deadmau5. There compositions are very original and pioneering due to the sounds they use which are often crafted by themselves.

Besides the foundations you need to have an overall vision for your music. This might come from a moment of inspiration or it could be something that happens when you really just sit and listen to your song and try to hear where it can go. What is it building to? What's the story you're telling? Listen to your favorite songs and do a lot of purposeful listening and learning around other people's music. Your first attempts will not be good. Getting stuck on one song for enormous amount of time will just hold you back. Move on quickly, try ideas, keep being creative, writing and recording. As your skill set grows you can always go back to those songs. No one creates at the highest levels all the time. If you sit there and wait for the creative juices to flow, believing that the only time you can work is when you feel creative will mean that nothing will get done. Regardless always create work through those times when you feel like you're not at your most creative. When you create things you will make mistakes and it is okay because you can learn from those mistakes. A lot of people are just getting a little bit too stressed and losing the fun in what they're doing. Before you know it all the music becomes too stressful and you're not in a very ideal or creative mindset to work. Often realizing that you're stressed can be quite difficult especially when you're working on something like music. If you're sitting away at the desk and you're frowning away and you're worried about it take a step back. Get out of the chair and get out of that area. Removing yourself from the environment can help you come up with different ways to overcome the problem. Then you can go back in and start working again. Try to spend as little time in the studio being stressed as possible so that you only associate sitting there with productive happy music.

Always keep developing and learning. You should be spending eighty percent of your time making music and twenty percent of your time going online finding tutorials and seeking out information. When you do seek out those tutorials seek them out for a specific purpose. Find relevant information and don't get caught into that trap of just watching endless amounts of everybody's opinion. The best way to retain information is for it to be purpose driven. You have a problem and you find a tutorial to solve it.

Finally, never compare yourself. When you see those superstar producers, you just see this rapid rise to fame. It seems like they're instantaneously successful and everyone knows who they are. But you don't see all the work that goes on behind the scenes. There's a one in a million person who's just brilliant right out the gate and the rest of us have to struggle, grow and create a lot of bad stuff. Maybe then some of that will be good and even then some of your stuff will still be bad. Often we can expect results a little bit too quickly.

Success in life that is truly worth having does take a long time to grow.

Embrace the journey, share ideas and be ready for the criticism you might take or the praise you might received. Music production is very much about the process and it's not just about the end goal of getting there and being successful. You need to enjoy the entire process, work your way through it and not get too hung up on wanting the success instantaneously. Given how fast everything moves these days it can be very easy to forget that skills take a long time to develop and there's nothing wrong with that. You should try to enjoy the process as much as possible.

Should You Study?

In the beginning of your music production journey you will need to spend more time on the learning just because there's so much that you need to get a foundational start. This leads to the question should you study music production? There are many institutes, colleges and universities offering really great course in music production.

Let's take a look at the advantages and disadvantages of enrolling to study. First, studying is a really good and easy way of meeting thousands of people. It sounds so cliche but it's so true. You genuinely won't get that experience sat in your bedroom no matter how many friends you may have at home. For example you might be a house music producer and you might need a singer on one of your tracks. If you're just sat at home you can maybe put up a Facebook post or have a look on some websites. But if you go to study, the likelihood is that one of your friends is going to be a singer. When you enrol to study you will be around a massive pool of production and performing talent that you can use which is so valuable. You can make relationships with these people, learn from them and start to make good music with them.

Next advantage is that studying music production is going to give you access to incredible equipment and facilities that you would normally not have access to without paying for. For example, normally you would never have the chance to mix on an SSL mixing desk or work in a studio with a control room with Pro Tools HD and a selection of professional microphones. Having the chance to get hands on experience working with that kind of stuff will help you determine whether it is something that you want to work in later on in life.

Next up the lecturers can be so so helpful in helping you to forge a career in music production. Criteria for lecturers is that they have to be actively participating in the industry to be able to lecture that subject at university. Therefore all of these lecturers are going to be people that have mixed and produced for bands that you will know. They're going to work for big companies that you will know and they're going to have really good connections. For you this could be very beneficial and open doors that otherwise wouldn't open. You could be an amazing mix engineer sat at home but if you don't know that guy that works for Universal Studios that can hook you up with a small band that needs a recording then you will be still sat at home.

Now the negatives. Studying is expensive, fees these days are on the rise and the only way that most students can afford them is with loans. The interest rates of these loans can be so high and they will keep on accumulating. Next, studying does not guarantee a job straight up after graduation because the industry is extremely competitive. However if you are going the extra mile, studying hard, working on projects outside of studies and making a name for yourself then it will give you a huge advantage. So many students go in with a minimal effort attitude and graduate with an average degree. Working hard will put you head and shoulders above the rest. Show up to the lectures and put in time and effort in outside of the lectures.

On a final note, almost all of the information in any course is available on the internet. This is going to be far less expensive and maybe quicker to access and digest. However you will require significant self discipline to follow through on that knowledge. Enrolling in a course will put you into a curriculum that will drive your progress forward. At the end of the day both studying at home and in a college or university have their own merits. The final decision based on your preferences and resources will be yours to make. The contents of this book should help you with your decisions in music production.

The Fundamentals of Music Production

Music Theory

Music theory is the backbone of producing great music. If you put regular time into learning and practicing it you will be rewarded so much in your creative journey.

As music producers we need an understanding of the fundamentals of music theory. We will go into music production techniques in more detail later on but for now let's get an understanding of the basic. The first step is knowing to how to find the notes on a piano. The music alphabet is the letters A through G and it just keeps repeating. When you look at the piano, you can see black keys and white keys. With the black keys you have groups of two and groups of three. The entire piano it's always groups of two and three. Now if you go to the first black key of a group of two and slide down to the left you have C. Now all you have to do is remember the alphabet C, D, E, F, G, A, B and you're back at C again. Then it keeps repeating on and on all the way up the scale.

The next thing I would advise you to learn is a key. The easiest keys to learn are C major and A minor. They use all of the white keys on the piano and by learning the key step by step you can easily figure out the chords that go with it. The A minor key starts on root note A and then uses all the following white keys until it cycles back around. The C major key starts with root note C and uses all the following white keys until it cycles back around. Major and minor keys are tools composers use to give their music a certain mood atmosphere or strength. Major and minor don't refer to single notes but to the spaces between notes and how far notes are from each other. These are measured in whole steps and half steps. Some combinations of whole and half steps create the sound of major and other combinations of whole and half steps create the sound of minor. Major usually sounds happy and triumphant. Whilst minor on the other hand often sounds bittersweet, sad and sometimes even scary. You can use each to its advantage depending on the emotion you are aiming to express through your music.

Now that you know some keys it's really easy to write melodies and chord progressions. Simply use only the keys in the scale. You can draw all of the notes in the scale into your DAW and mute them so you have a little guide. The easiest chord to use is the triad and it uses three keys. For most chords you would play the root note, skip one, play one, skip one and play one. So in the case of a C major triad you would use the keys C, E and G. You can add a seventh key on the top for extra harmony and create a seventh chord by adding the B. For the A minor triad use the keys A, C, E. To add the seventh use the key G. Another nice thing you can do is copying the root notes one octave down and you will get a chord that is a bit thicker. Maybe give them a slightly different rhythm to make it a bit more interesting. You can look up more chords online and try different variations in your music. Play the chords by ear and trust your instincts. To progress from chord to chord you can draw the root key in first and then try different variations on the top.

Once you have a good chord progression and bass line you can work on your melody. It doesn't necessarily have to be in this order. Music can start in any way. One of the simplest ways to write a melody is to first hum it. You can then get the rhythm of it correct by recording in your humming or drawing in notes on one key. Alternatively if you have a midi keyboard connected you could play it in. Next you need to tidy up the timing and then start to choose what keys you want each note to fall on. Make sure you stay within the scale of the key your working in and then it will be good to go. What I again suggest is to draw in all the notes of the scale and then mute them so you have a visual reference of what keys you can use. The melody should be consistent and catchy. Don't try to be too clever and switch it up all the time. Of course you want some variation to keep it interesting but maintain the essence of the song. Most popular music is very simple. A cool thing what many producers do is to shift the melody onto a different instrument. Listen to Calvin Harris songs, he does that a lot. Or check out some of the work of KSHMR who is great at switching up his melodies every few bars.

Science of Sound

As an aspiring music producer it's important to understand the fundamentals of how sound actually works. Figuratively speaking sound is a wave it, that is it's a vibration and travels through a medium such as air or water. Imagine if you drop a rock into a bucket of water it will disturb the surface of the water and create ripples or waves which travel away from the impact. The ripples cause the height of the water to change going up and down as the waves move away from the splash. These waves are visible with our eyes and have a number of properties. They have a maximum point called a crest and a minimum point called a trough. They have a wavelength which is the distance from a particular crest to the next one. They have an amplitude which is the distance from the top of a crest to the bottom of a trough. They have a frequency which is the number of waves that pass a fixed point per second.

In essence sound waves are similar. Imagine if you clap your hands in a quiet room it will disturb the air and cause ripples of air to move away from your hands. The clap disturbs the air molecules near your hands. These molecules then bounce into other nearby molecules and so on. The disturbance moves through the air like a wave in water. Sound waves create changes in air pressure causing particles to be bunched together or spread apart. There are not visible but our ears can hear them. When the waves reach our ears the air pressure goes up and down and this makes our eardrums go in and out in harmony. Our brain analyzes these signals and interprets them as sound.

Noise and notes are both a combination of sound waves at various different frequencies. The difference between them is that a note features a pattern of waves that repeats in an ordered way. Whilst a note consists of individual ripples that do not repeat and so are disordered. When an object moves it disturbs the surrounding air which will ripple out as sound waves. If the vibration of the object is fast with a repeating pattern then the sound waves will be more uniformly spaced and regular, like a string. The air particles will be squeezed together tightly into evenly spaced waves. To the ear these will be heard as notes with a distinct pitch. However if you hit a hammer on a surface you will hear a noise consisting of unrelated frequencies with no repeating pattern. To the ear this will be heard as a noise with no defined pitch.

As long as the pattern of waves repeats itself the sound produced will be a note regardless of how complicated the individual ripples are. Incidentally musical notes don't necessarily have be made by musical instruments. Anything that creates a vibration which disturbs the air in a uniform pattern will produce a note. For example the sounds of a Formula One race car engine or of a cat create a note. Smooth and even sound waves are created from instruments like a flute sound. Whilst more complex wave patterns that sound much richer are created by instrument like a violin.

Soundwaves generally have four main qualities. Frequency which determines the pitch, wave shape which determines the timbre, amplitude which determines the volume and phase which determines how sound waves interact. If a string vibrates back and forth two hundred times a second it's causing or emitting two hundred sound waves per second. The number of sound waves that pass a fixed point per second or the number of times a string vibrates per second is called the frequency and it is measured in hertz (hZ). If our string is vibrating at two hundred times per second then its frequency will be 200 Hertz. When you play middle A the frequency is 440 Hertz again this means the string is vibrating back and forth 440 times per second. Therefore frequency and wavelength determine the pitch of the sound.

Because all sound travels at the speed of sound which is roughly 343 m/s through air, waves with a shorter wavelength will arrive at our ears more frequently than longer waves. The pitch of a note is determined by its frequency. Changing the shape of the sound wave while keeping the same frequency will change how the note sounds and that is defined as its timbre. Sounds can have the same frequency but a different sound due to the wave being shaped differently / timbre. Wave shaping is done extensively in electronic music and this allows you to make a note sound much more interesting than a plain old boring sine wave.

The human ear can generally hear frequencies between 20 and 20,000 Hertz. Amplitude is a measurement of the amount of change in air pressure caused by a sound wave. It is a measure of the distance between the maximum and minimum of that wave and is measured in meters. All other things being equal if you increase the amplitude of the sound waves then you increase the volume of the sound. The perceived volume of the note depends on its frequency. Human hearing is more sensitive to notes in the middle range at around 2,000 to 5,000 Hertz. At the extreme bottom or extreme top of the range even when playing at the same amplitude a note will be perceived as quieter. This is why bass guitars or double basses always sound quieter than the rest of the band and while you hear the higher pitched instruments over the rest of the orchestra. Low-pitched instruments have to be played harder to get the same level of volume as higher pitched instruments. Keep this in mind when you are mixing.

The most common way of measuring loudness is with decibels. The decibel scale is used to compare the relative intensities of any two sounds. It is a measure of the intensity of a sound relative to the threshold of human hearing. Zero decibels is the softest level that a human can hear. The average level of speaking voices is around sixty decibels. Sounds above eighty five decibels can permanently damage your ears if you're exposed to them for a long time. Always wear inner ear protection if you are going to be exposed to loud sounds for a long period of time. Most ear damage is irreversible.

When you hit a piano key at first you will hear a loud ringing as the hammer hits the string and then there is an immediate fall in volume as the note is sustained. This variation of amplitude over time is referred to as the sound envelope. The sound envelope is made up of four parts. The attack which is the initial strike of the note which usually creates the loudest part of the sound. The decay which is the drop in intensity immediately after the attack. The sustain which is the steady-state sound of the note as it's sustained and the release which is when the key is released and the note stops sounding. The envelope of the sound helps determine an instrument. For example drums usually have a fast attack, decay, sustain and release. Whilst strings have a slow attack with longer decay, sustain and release times.

Digital Sound

The process of capturing sound in a digital format is called sampling. A sample is an aesthetic representation of a waveform in time. The amount of samples that are recorded per second is defined as sample rate. If we sample a twenty kilohertz frequency with a sample rate of twenty kilohertz the result will be one sample per completed cycle. In order to capture the full range of the cycle we need to have a sampling rate that is double the frequency that we're sampling. This is because when sampling, the highest frequencies can cause aliasing errors and various other problems. Therefore we need to filter off the highest frequencies with a low-pass filter. In order to compensate for the cut off we need to have a sample rate of at least forty kilohertz to properly capture a twenty kilohertz frequency.

We can say that sampling is the process of recording an amplitude value in time and it is captured during a process called quantization. Digital recording systems will capture samples at a specific resolution across the amplitude axis.

With a higher resolution the digital representation of the waveform will be much more accurate. The bit depth of the recording equipment being used will determine this. Having a higher bit depth will allow a greater dynamic range to be captured. A 16-bit recording has a theoretical dynamic range of 96 dB whereas 24 bit audio has a theoretical dynamic range of 144 dB. Mixing with the higher bit depth is great for recording very dynamic sources such as an orchestra which can go from very quiet to very loud in its dynamic range. Audio interfaces nowadays can support sampling rates of up to 192 kilohertz for much higher audio quality and processing options.

The filters and the analogue to digital converters that are being used by an audio interface are really crucial in determining what the quality of the recorded audio will be. Having a higher bit depth will make mixing processing more accurate and also offer a lot higher resolution when using effects such as EQ, reverb, compression, etc. Everything will sound much better at the higher sample rate. In fact, many plugins feature up sampling techniques to internally work at higher sample rates. Higher sample rates however will stress your computer a lot more so you'll definitely need some more processing power. If you don't have that keep in mind that you won't be able to add as many tracks or plugins as you were used to at lower sample rates.

Build Your Dream Studio: Computer Music

Building a studio might seem unrealistic when you think of those big studios used by the professionals. You might think that achieving the same results that you would in a full fledged professional studio is near impossible. However with the fast development power of the modern producing world it is becoming easier than ever to make high quality music from your home studio. The key to building your first studio is to always utilize what you have. It isn't necessarily about having the very best equipment but rather knowing how to use what you have effectively. If your on a budget you can still get great equipment at an affordable price. Know what your budget is and then it's up to you to allocate your money appropriately. Let's take a look at what equipment you need to set up your first studio.

A word of warning first. One of the major problems that we have in the modern home recording era is that there is so much gear available. This is a great blessing but the curse of it is there's so much available that we think that there's something better out there and that we should be using everybody's using different gear. We watch an interview with our favorite producer and we say man they use those plugins or those monitors I got to get those. There's nothing wrong with wanting to use the gear that your friends or your heroes or whatever use. The problem is is when we always change our gear so often we never get to really learn it. We never get to really master our gear, we never really get to learn the nuances and the details of what our gear can do. If you keep changing your tools your going to keep going back to learning now you're not thinking about music making. Get something commit to it, use it and make a lot of music with it.

Computer

The first piece of equipment you will need is a computer. I'm not going to get into the Mac versus PC discussion because both offer really great options. Today's computers can handle so much more and I'm sure that what you have is perfectly fine to get started.

If you don't really need to or plan to travel with your computer often then always choose a desktop computer. For the price and speed a desktop computer will be a much better option. In order to fit the components of a laptop into that small space manufactures make compromises. Whatever you decide on the fundamental things to look out for are the same.

Some of the things you should look out for are ram, hard drive space and fast, reliable processors. For the processor choose an i7 or if you have the budget an i9. The best manufacturer and one you should always go with is an Intel processor. For ram/memory, 8gb would be the starting point and if you can afford to choose 16gb. Although in most computers you will always have the option to upgrade the memory later on. When selecting a hard drive make sure that you have one that is fast enough to handle reading multiple tracks at the same time. Ideally you need to have at least 7200 rpm or better even a SSD which will also save on the battery life of your laptop. In addition make sure that you have enough hard disk space with 500gb being the bear minimum. Even one terabyte of space still isn't really adequate because you will run out of space eventually so try to go above that. Also you should regularly back up your data to an external hard drive. For your screen preferably go for a 17-inch and if you have an external monitor you can hook that up via HDMI which is great for having one screen for mixing and another for arrangement. Also make sure that you have a backlit keyboard so you can easily see your keyboard in low lighting which is in most studios.

Apple with their MacBook series offer extended warranty and are known for using quality components that last long and are durable. When something is broken they can probably fix it quite easily and also they still work great over five years on from buy date. Acer, Lenovo and Samsung have some gaming laptops that are designed to withstand heavy workloads and that's good for music production. Take in mind the specifications outlined and see what is available for your budget. Be sure to also research any computer thoroughly and check out all the reviews before you invest.

Software

Next up you will need some software or Digital Audio Workstation (DAW). This will be your command center and it is where all your recordings will go and is where you work on your music. There are a lot of options out there. Now if you're running a Mac this decision is very simple, start with GarageBand. It's a free software that will familiarize you with recording, mixing and producing. There are many more different Digital Audio Workstations out there and I will cover the bigger ones here. Overall the best DAW is the one that you can work the quickest and be the most comfortable with. Don't listen to what everybody else says, that you need to use Ableton or Logic or whatever. Every DAW has its own strengths and weaknesses and if there was one DAW for everybody then everybody would use it. If your not sure you can download a demo of one of the DAW's and test it out before you buy.

Pro Tools

Pro Tools is still regarded as the industry standard digital audio workstation at the moment so if you're looking for the best of the best then this is definitely it. The majority of professional recording studios are using it so if you have some type of knowledge of it then that's a great advantage to have because it will make your future studio experiences a lot more easier.

It is well known for rendering great quality audio and is a seamless choice for large recordings of instruments. It's also got 64-bit architecture which means that it will take advantage of any of your computer's RAM / 4 gigabyte as well and it's Windows and Mac compatible so it doesn't matter what computer you have.

Pro Tools is definitely aimed at professional there's number of reasons for this and the first is that there's a very limited number of stock plugins. This is intentional because they're expecting that people are going to have their own third-party plugins and hardware that are used in a traditional analog studio. However it does support most third party plugins and integrates easily with hardware recording equipment. The stock plugins that come with it are exceptional, they're very high quality and sound great. The software is very user customizable, you can change a lot of the parameters to your taste and what you like to see on a daily basis. Large studios particularly only use Pro Tools for tracking bands and mixing but there are still many composers that use it for songwriting.

Currently it is on version 12 and the is available as a monthly subscription of $25 per month for one year or for one payment of $299. Famous users include, Timbaland, Dr Dre, Paul Epworth, Pharrell Williams and many more.

Logic Pro X

Logic Pro X has come on the scene as being a real heavy hitter for electronic music producers and even producers that are working with bands. If you're upgrading from GarageBand, Logic is a very natural progression. Building on the basics of GarageBand it is a fully featured DAW that can do just about everything Pro Tools and every other DAW does. You get full multitrack mixing and you can insert all the plugins you want. Plus there's a 64-bit application to support audio unit plugins at 64 bit rates. The interface is really to navigate, for the singer-songwriter especially and that makes it really easy to make music.

The stock plugins are really great. In particular the amps and pedals which model the features of real amps and sound great. For singers the flex pitch is a great stock plug in which allows you to fix the pitch and timing of any audio. A very unique virtual drummer takes the concept of virtual drums to be even more user-friendly inside the DAW application. You can choose the kit you want and build it and customize it to be loud, soft whatever you want. Then you've got plenty of loops ordered in different sound types, instruments, key and bpm.

At the moment Logic Pro X is exclusively only available for Mac. The price point of Logic Pro X is around $199 which is super reasonable for what you're getting from the software. Famous users include, Hardwell, Calvin Harris, Swedish House Mafia, Alesso and many more.

Ableton Live

Ableton Live offers seamless music production and excellent onboard plugins. It really sets itself apart with the algorithms it uses to manipulate sound in general. Whether you're into sound design, composition work, production for bands or something a little more outside of the box then your options with Ableton really are unlimited.

The concept of collections to the browser is a great user friendly option to pull together all of your favorite sounds, samples, presets, plugins and projects all into one place. The new capture function allows you to easily save performances even if you weren't recording at the time which makes it really easy to capture spontaneity. You can play loops along with your session and quickly scroll through them as they will be played in BPM with the rest of the session. This is very practical if you're hunting for loops and trying to build your dance groove within your arrangement. You can also create quite complex mixing structures.

The stock plug ins are really high quality, you can create very digital sounds or very analog style sounds. Or you can create really warm smooth sounds or really aggressive sounds, it's all very diverse. They have several different analog distortion boxes from a warm crisp overdrive sound to a modern aggressive distortion and much more. Then there are a bunch of different delay devices from analogue tape delay to digital hardware delay. There are many more great stock plug ins to explore inside, just dive in they are really user friendly.

Ableton is really popular with EDM producers and from a live standpoint it is unreal the things that you can do it. It reacts really well with CPU intensive plugins and it still manages to keep a low latency most of the times. The full version rounds out at about $229. There are also lite version available for a cheaper price. Famous users include, Flume, Skirllex, Diplo, Bauuer and many more.

Fl Studio

Fl Studio started out under the name fruity loops and they released in 2018 a Mac version so it's now available on Windows and on the Mac. FL Studio has a little bit of an image problem. A lot of people don't take FL Studio seriously because it looks different to a lot of other DAW'S. Some might say it looks a little bit basic or amatuer. But don't mistake it's look for the power it possesses.

The interface is really user friendly and has some powerful tools. The pattern roll is a really cool feature which allows you to quickly program in a complete drum loop. Normally this could take you hours of time spent editing in the piano roll or otherwise trying to record your loops in live. If your computer is low on RAM the step editing mode lets you input notes by a computer keyboard or MIDI without having to record anything live which significantly reduces MIDI latency.

FL studio comes with a great set of stock plugins that can be used for mixing, engineering and mastering your music. With these you will easily be able to achieve very professional sounding music results. There are more than enough included to cater for your requirements without having to invest more cash in buying other unnecessary plug-ins. Then there are the virtual synthesizers which include subtractive, additive, drum, granular and even frequency modulation. These are great for giving you the opportunity to create unique sounds in a variety of music genres.

One of the greatest things about FL Studio is that it comes with a variety of different sample packs that you can use to program strings, choirs, brass, woodwinds and many more different types of instruments. The browser window also makes them extremely easy to preview. All you have to do is click the sample file with your mouse and you'll get a preview of the sound. This makes searching for the perfect kick or snare sound a smooth and effortless process. Finally the sample editor is an awesome tool for those of you who want to produce glitch music or music with a lot of edits in. This will save you literally hours of time from manually cutting stretching and pitching audio files. It really is a powerful feature and you can hear it in a lot songs that have these pitch chop vocal drops.

The price of FL Studio starts at $199 for the basic package and upto $899 for the full package with all plugins and synthesizers. Famous users include, Martin Garrix, Porter Robinson, Afrojack and many more.

Reason

Reason by Propellerheads has a great sound design engine that lets you easily combine many instruments to create amazing sounds from the stock sounds. Some of your favorite songs are probably made from stock Reason sounds. The user interface is really easy to use with customizable options and great performance. Writing songs and drawing in automation is a breeze.

Inside it has some really great synths. Europa is a really awesome and incredibly powerful modern synth that uses almost no processor power. The vocal synth is excellent at choir type effects and then clanging the tuned percussion is awesome. The piano is fantastic and the samplers inside make it really easy for adding in other sample instruments. You can of course combine all those instruments together to create really cool and unique sounds. It uses hardly any processing power to do that. Also if you want you can run Reason in the background of another DAW so it becomes almost like this epice VST. In addition to the stock sounds Reason 10 provides full VST support.

The price of reason is currently $299 with the option of a free trial for thirty days. Famous users include, DJ Mustard, Mike Will Made It, The Prodigy and many more.

Plug Ins and Virtual Synthesizers

Plug ins and virtual synthesizers are made by third party developers to be used in your chosen DAW. Most DAW's will also have their own stock plugins and synths for standard things such as compression, EQ, reverb, chorus, panning, etc. There are so many different kinds of plug ins that can be used to change, enhance or fix the sound. Adding some to your collection will give you more power. But before you do that make sure your buying it for the right reasons. Don't get the latest plug in because it is hot now. If the stock plug in does the job then stick with it. Anway, let's take a look at some of the most popular plug ins.

Waves
Waves are currently one of the most famous and respected developers of plug ins and signal processors in the music production industry. So many of the world's top producers are using them. They are known and well respected for very high quality and are used in every aspect of music production from mixing and mastering to production, live sound and more.

They are particularly well known for reverb, compression, EQ, limiting, noise reduction. The quality does come at a price but there are many different bundles available to cater for your requirements. For compatibility they offer versions in VST, TDM, RTAS and AU formats,

Izoptope

Izotope are well respected in the music production industry as offering great sound to help producers and engineers seamlessly improve their music. They have designed award winning software and plugins. Ozone 8 is one of their most popular plugins. It is a full mastering suite with intelligent signal processing, signal shaping, tone balancing and more. It aims to provide the user with a full set of mastering tools and can be used in RTAS, AAX, VST, AU or as a stand alone unit.

Another of their popular plugins is Izotope Trash. This is one of the most advanced distortion units available. It can combine powerful, multi band, dual stage and filtered distortion units. This will give warmth, crunch or hardcore distortion to your sounds. Highly recommend for guitars and drums.

Fabfilter

Offer plugins for reverb, EQ, compression, mid side, limiting and more. Known for being user friendly and having high fidelity output. Powerful and innovative. They are available to try out in demo version first and buy late if you like. www.splice.com also offer rent to own options.

Valhalla Room

A clean and realistic reverb. Features twelve reverb algorithms that produce a variety of natural reverberation sounds. Sounds range from light ambience in rooms to huge halls and vast spaces. All algorithms can be altered to the users preferences.

Guitar Rig

Guitar Rig is plug in used to model amplifiers and effects from guitar pedals. It is primarily aimed to be used with guitars and basses but can work well with various other signal inputs. Very user friendly and offers a lot of different combinations to produce really cool sounds.

Melodyne

Celemony Melodyne is an excellent plug in used for changing and correcting the pitch of sounds. Typically this is used on vocals but could be used on other pitched instruments. For example if you recorded in a vocal and there are some notes that are a bit off key or off time then you can easily fix that with Melodyne. This also works on chords as well as single notes. It is very transparent and can turn an out of tune vocal into a pitch perfect one. However it makes life easier if the original vocal is well performed and recorded in the first place. Supported in VST, AU and stand alone units.

Sugar Bytes Effectrix

Sugar Bytes Effectrix is a multi effects plug in used for sequenced sound manipulations. It allows you to mash up or tweek your beats, create new patterns, reverse, stretch, delay and alter your sounds in upto sixteen different ways.

VSTIS

Virtual studio instruments (VSTIS) allow you to add in powerful software instruments into your DAW. This will allow you to utilize anything from modern synthesizers to real world instruments. All DAW's will come with a few stock DAW's but these are usually quite basic compared to what is out there. Let's take a look at some of the best ones.

Komplete

Brings all of the Native Instruments, instrument and effect plugins together into one comprehensive package ready to run as a standalone instrument or inside the DAW of your choice. Offers a huge library of synthesizers, sampled instruments and expansion packs with over 25,000 preset sounds and fifty instruments/processors. This really is a solution to every aspect of sound and includes the following. Kontakt, an award winning sampler which is great for loading drum hits and multi samples to create your own instruments. There are also excellent sound libraries offered with this. You got pianos, strings, basses, drums, orchestras and more all at your fingertips. Massive, a very popular synthesizer which can easily create digital and analogue style sounds. Reaktor which allows you to program in your own instruments and effects, endless possibilities. Guitar Rig Pro, used for awesome guitar style effects. Maschine, a drum creation and programming tool. FM8 advanced FM synthesizer and much more. Also included in the package is a hardware keyboard controller.

Serum

Serum is a groundbreaking virtual synthesizer that has become an industry standard in the music production world. If you are in any way into sound design and all that stuff this is hands down one of the best synthesizers you can get for the money. The quality of the sound is unbelievable. It has your basic oscillators to create the wave table sounds and you can also drag and drop any sound into the oscillators. Plus you have a sub oscillator for your bass and a noise oscillator so you can add some external noise. These will both help to fill out your sounds. The filter options are really great with so many different types available. You can filter, add envelopes, lfos, effects and much more. The matrix routing options are really powerful. Included are a lot of high quality presets that you can easily access across different categories. The sounds that are included are really great or you can easily make your own from scratch or just work on the existing ones.

Sylenth

Sylenth is a really popular virtual synthesizer that is used by many of the biggest names in music production. It's good for pads, leads, arpeggiators, baselines and more. The interface is really flexible and allows you to easily adjust sounds and parameters. You can route things really easy, for example to set up lfo's or envelope modulations. It also comes with a built in compressor, reverb, delays, equalizer, chorus, phase and distortion. I highly recommend this if you want to start producing electronic music because you will get some great sounds out of it.

Nexus

Nexus is a really powerful Rom sampler with some amazing sounds and has the option for adding on sound banks from famous producers. It features an extremely efficient screen which by default displays the different sound banks and all of the presets inside of them. This makes it easy to find the sound you are looking for.

On the interface are six main sections, the first section is the filter modifier and this section includes the envelope cutoff and resonance along with the standard ADSR envelopes. There is a master filter which can control the master cutoff and resonance of the sound. Controlling these knobs along with automation is a great way to add flavor to any track. Nexus also includes its own effects units which are delay and reverb. The quality of these are quite high nice so you don't have to worry about adding another plugin to your mixer channel. Additional tabs include the modulation arpeggiator and trance gate. The standard version comes with many great presets or you can add expansion packs.

Spire

Spire is a virtual synthesizer that has a really powerful sound and works well in dance music and hip hop. It comes with five banks and you can also get more packs online or creating your own sounds is very easy. There are four oscillators which have numerous wavetables available to be detuned, mashed and smashed together in harmony. Then there are some awesome filters with a multitude of different ones available for filtering your sounds. The effects section has five effects including shaping, phase, chorus, delay and reverb. These are really great and you probably won't need any extra plug ins. Finally, the routing options of are excellent and overall the synth is super easy to use and produces great sounds.

Omnisphere

Omnisphere is a virtual instrument that has both a huge synth engine as well as an enormous bank of sampled sounds. It has almost endless sound design capabilities and therefore it is great for composers and sound designers but really it can be used for any style of music. It comes with a vast library of over 12,000 sounds in almost every kind of style from EDM to soundscapes. It is also very easy to either create your own sounds from scratch or make variations on any of the included patches. You can choose how deep you want to go in your own sound design you can use the easy interface for fast workflow or go deep into custom modulation. If you invest in it you will want a powerful computer with a large hard drive because it is demanding in space and performance.

Build Your Dream Studio: Hardware

Audio Interface

In order to send the sounds from your computer to speakers or headphones and also to convert the analogue signal from your microphone or instrument your going to need an audio interface. Personally I use an Apogee duet as my main audio interface but there's just so many great options out there. Universal Audio is a big favorite but I think the best option for those of you who are starting out is the Scarlett Solo from Focusrite. It's $99 and it comes with two free software options, Pro Tools or Ableton Live Lite. It features one microphone input and one instrument input and it records at really high sample rates which will be perfect for your home studio recording needs.

Headphones

Next you will need a set of headphones. Medium priced headphones will be fine, you don't necessarily need the most expensive headphones. I recommend you visit a professional audio store and test out a few different sets there based on your budget. Also take a look at the reviews of them before you invest. To help you more,check out the top five best studio headphones that I recommend. These are based on their price, quality, durability and more.

Sony MDR 75006

The Sony MDR 75006 have been around in the industry for a little while which make them a trusted and certified option for the music producer who is looking for strong, lasting and quality headphones. From a design perspective these headphones are closed off at the back so you will barely notice any external noise interference. In turn this will help you to be more focused on your music. They come in an all black finish with a comfortable, padded headband that sits softly on your head. This helps them to stay on your head whilst ensuring a higher level of comfort. Storing them in the included soft case is really easy because the ear cups are also foldable and so you can maintain their original look. The cable attachment is extremely long and durable so you can still be quite mobile. The MDR 75006 have been greatly praised for their ability to output a well matched audio from the left and the right drivers. This is really important because you can feel an accurate localization and enjoy having a better stereo image.

Audio Technica ATHM70X

The audio technica ATHM70X are closed-back professional studio monitor headphones that combine a reasonable price with a really strong performance. From a design perspective these headphones feature a stylish all-black well-built construction that consists of 90 degree swiveling ear cups and a sturdy plastic headband that is wrapped in a soft material. This will reduce pressure points on your head so you won't feel tight. Included with them are three detachable cables including a coiled cable, two straight cables and a 1/4 inch screw on an adapter plus a carrying case as well so you will be equipped with everything needed. The sound quality is exceptionally balanced in the lows and highs. They also have an excellent sound isolation. Since these headphones have a fold flat design it means that you won't have any difficulties in terms of portability and storage.

BeyerDynamic DT 1990 Pro

The BeyerDynamic DT 1990 Pro are among one of the most popular studio headphones in the music production industry. In fact you have probably seen this model come up many times if you were searching for headphones. From a design perspective they feature an open back all black or all grey construction that is made of strong metal that is cased in padding / foam. This make them both long lasting and very comfortable. Both the headband and the ear sets can be easily replaced. This is great since most headphones don't have that option. Included are also two pairs of cables that are a straight cable and a coiled cable along with a strong, hard case to offer a secure storage. The sound produced is very detailed and accurate from the left and the right stereo field. Many users have also stated that the low end is really well defined, whilst the mids and highs are very well produced as well. However the isolation isn't quite as good since they have an open design that is primarily designed for mixes and mastering. But this is quite normal and won't be a setback.

Bowers & Wilkins P9

The Bowers & Wilkins P9 is an excellent option for music production headphones. From a design they look really cool and are set in an aluminum frame with real leather headband and ear cups. This gives them an expensive look and also feels extremely comfortable on your head. Adjusting them and finding an ideal position is very easy and they will lock in place allowing you to wear them for long periods of time without feeling discomfort. They come with a detachable four foot cable, remote and an really long cable for listening at home. Regarding sound quality they do an excellent job in producing an accurate representation with clarity and would never disappoint with their performance. Overall they look both as good as they perform.

Sennheiser HD 800 S

The Sennheiser HD 800 S are premium headphones which are great for music producers who want to invest in a pair of headphones that are armed with everything required. From a design perspective they feature an open back design that is made of strong metal and comfortable padding. The headband is covered with several layers of resonance damping polymers that play a crucial role in minimizing vibrations. This basically means that they will absorb any unwanted resonance energy while enhancing the high and the low frequency range so the end result will be of a very high quality. They come with two cables including a four pin XLR balanced cable that will provide a better audio quality from sources with balanced outputs. Sound performance wise they have a full detailed sound with minimal distortion. Give them a try and assure yourself that they have great quality.

Speakers

If you decide to use speakers instead of headphones than that is a good idea because you will be able to listen to a more accurate representation of the audio. Speakers can produce lower frequencies more accurately and are reproducing audio in a three dimensional plane. It is a good idea to use a combination of speakers and headphones. You want to always be testing your mixes on both and then striking a balance between the two. This will help your mixes to translate well across the different systems. Also in some situations your room or lifestyle might limit your options. For example maybe you travel a lot. In this situation i would advise you to produce most of your music with headphones and then at the mixing and sound design stages you can move over to speakers. Now, let's take a look at the top five best studio monitors

Mackie CR 3
The Mackie CR 3 is a pair of compact studio monitors that combine excellent audio quality for an affordable price. From a design perspective they feature a wooden construction that is finished with a green and black color combination which looks very stylish. Regardless of where you put them they will look good. The speakers can output fifty watts of power whilst the audio frequency response ranges from 80 to 20 kilohertz. They come with a number of accessories which allows you to connect a computer, smartphone or media player. Another great thing about these speakers is that they come with isolation pads which will drastically minimize the build-up of any boomy low frequencies and enhance your overall listening focus.

M-Audio AV 42
The M-Audio AV 42 are an ideal option for most small home studios. From a design perspective they feature a compact construction that is mostly made of MDF and this cuts weight drastically. In addition they have a black matte finish which makes them very look stylish indeed. They can be connected

to most of your gear including, tablets, computers and mixers. The frequency response is from 75 to 20,000 Hertz and the four inch woofer will reproduce a great amount of bass so you can feel every audio track in depth. Overall they produce great quality audio and will never restrict you in terms of connectivity.

Yamaha HS 8
The Yamaha HS 8 have quickly become a first choice of speaker for most professional music studios. From a design perspective they feature an attractive sleek white MDF design. On the speakers are controls that include room control and high frequency trim. The room control switch helps to compensate for the build up of low end frequencies which can cause exaggeration. This usually happens if you've placed the speakers to close to walls or in the corners. Whilst the mid and high trim help to tame excess high frequency build up which is common in most home studios. Included you can find one XLR and a 1/4 inch TRS phone jack input that can accept both balanced or unbalanced signals. The amplifier unit will ensure that each speaker delivers a high-resolution sound as well as a flat response across your entire room. They also have a noise reduction technology which results in effective reduction of noise by up to six decibels.

KRK Rokit 5
The KRK Rokit are a great set of speakers from KRK systems at an affordable price. They have a number of different sized models but the five inch speaker is going to be perfect for most people. If you need more low end response, the addition of subwoofers can help. From a design perspective they come in a really, solid design with a smooth contour. On the back of the speakers are a main volume knob for setting output level without having to overloaded the mixer. Also then you have a

high frequency level adjustment knob which is pretty common in speakers. This will help to compensate rooms that cause excess high frequency build up. You might notice this when you mix. Things will sound crisp and bright punchy but when you take the mix outside of that room it sounds muffled. Using a control like this allows you to cut out some of the high frequencies because your room is giving you more high frequencies than you need. The speakers feature standard RCA connections and balanced TRS connections which can connect to a variety of equipment types. These speakers are self powered / active monitors so you can just plug them straight into the wall. Overall they produce a high quality and accurate sound for an affordable price.

Midi Keyboard

If your good at piano or you want to be able to perform your own melodies then a midi keyboard is the best way to record your ideas into your DAW. Just plug it into your computer via USB cable or through a midi interface. Most audio interfaces have midi capability but if not it is easy to get a decent midi connector for an affordable price. Signals sent from the keyboard will tell the computer what notes are being pressed. In most DAW's you can adjust how responsive the keyboard is. For keyboards I recommend models from M-audio or Native Instruments. You can choose the keys to be semi weighted or fully weighted. The latter is more expensive but will feel much more like a piano and be easier to play. In addition if you want to control other parameters in your DAW you can use a midi controller such as a beatpad. Ableton have a really awesome step controller which allows you to assign various parameters to the grid buttons. This is really powerful for performances or recording in automation movements.

Microphone

If your recording instruments or vocals you will need a microphone. Now let's say you're a singer or recording vocals and the quality of vocals is really important to you. If this is the case well then you need to understand the different types of microphones that are available. Most will fit into one of three different categories, ribbon microphones, condenser microphones or dynamic microphones. Ribbon microphones are more rare and you are less likely to see them and much less likely to afford them. Condenser microphones are the best for high quality studio recordings. They are incredibly sensitive to sources and produce accurate results and are particularly good in the high frequencies. In the majority of situations condenser microphones will reproduce a better quality of recording than a dynamic microphone would. Dynamic microphones are more durable and less sensitive therefore making them more suitable for live performances. However this is not to say that dynamic microphones are only useful for live music. In fact the Shure SM57 is probably one of the most used microphones for music recordings. But in a lot of cases especially when recording vocals you're going to want a good condenser microphone.

The price of condenser microphones can get astronomically high. But don't worry, you don't have to break the bank to get something decent. For under $200 the Bluebird from Blue Microphones offers great sound quality. As your studio evolves and you start adding things like preamps this microphone is only going to become more powerful. Another great budget option is the Samson CO1. Now if you know a little bit about condenser microphones you will surely of heard of the Neuman U87. It is widely regarded as one of the best microphones that money can buy. It is expensive but for the price you will get value for money. The sound quality is high and high frequencies are particularly well produced. This makes it a great microphone for recording acoustic guitars or as a drum overhead mic or even just a general room microphone. In addition it is also a favourite for recording with vocals.

Other options are the Audio Technica models who have a great range of condenser microphones that have a lot of similarities to the Neuman U87. In addition the Audio Technica series offers a couple of advanced features which make their application very multi-purpose. First of all they have multi patterned microphones which simply put means that there are a few different settings that determine how the microphone picks up sound. It can be an omnidirectional pattern, a cardioid pattern and a bi-directional pattern which basically just adds to the versatility of the microphones.

Last but not least it's worth mentioning again the Sure SM57 and Shure SM58. Yes, these are dynamic microphones but they are incredibly popular because they are both durable and produce high quality results. The SM57 is usually used for female vocals and higher frequency sounds whilst the SM58 is usually used for male vocals and lower frequency sounds. If you are looking for a great bass drum microphone the Shure Egg drum microphone is an excellent choice. In addition these microphones will work well in the studio and on the live stage. Shure microphones are going to last for a long time, produce great results and won't break the bank.

With your microphones you will want to get a couple of accessories including a mic stand, XLR cables and a pop filter. Always use XLR cables, they are balanced which means there will be less noise. In addition invest in high quality cables, it's no use having a decent microphone with a rubbish cable. The pop filter is going to help protect the microphone from popping sounds that are created by P and S sounds. You can also add in a sound shield or an acoustic shield will help to eliminate sound from bouncing off other surfaces in your room and traveling into the microphone. This offers a more affordable and easier solution to sound treating a room with acoustic treatment and bass traps. It simply sits behind the microphone.

Hey, I hope you're enjoying this book....if so please share your feedback with a good review.

Acoustic Treatment

If you do decide to treat your room then you can look into acoustic treatment solutions. Often you will find that when you play back your mixes in your home studio that it doesn't sound quite right. You fiddle with the settings in the mix thinking it might be that but it's to no avail. You might think to blame your studio monitors themselves or the microphone you used to record. But often times in a home recording studio that's not the real issue you're dealing with. In many cases the culprit is sound reflections.

When sound travels and bounces off a surface it ultimately affects the way you hear it. As a home recording music producer you're probably working in less than ideal conditions. Any flat walls, ceilings, hardwood or tiled floors and countertops can all be reflective surfaces which sound waves will bounce off of making the audio you hear have reflections. If your recording in any square or rectangular room with parallel walls, similar to the rooms in most people's houses then your playback is at the risk of comb filtering. When two or more sound waves reflect off of a surface and crash into each other it causes a delay. That may sound like a cool idea but it actually affects the way you hear the audio. As the sound waves wind up hitting your ears at different times they also hit each other at the wrong time causing interference and cancelation. This can cause your music to sound weak or muddled but it is most likely just an effect of the room you're working in and not necessarily your mixing technique.

Absorption and Diffusion

So if something as basic as parallel walls is affecting your mixing how do you change it? No one expects you to remodel your house, a much easier solution is acoustic treatment. To start with there are two types of acoustic treatment to consider when thinking about your space, absorption and diffusion. With absorption sound waves become absorbed and are unable to reflect off the walls. Whereas diffusion breaks up the sound waves before they can collide with each other. For now let's talk about absorption. That's the option most people think of when talking about acoustic treatment. We've all seen photos of professional recording studios with the foam panels on the wall. Absorbing sound before it has a chance to reflect off the walls will eliminate a lot of the problems with those unwanted reflections. The best way to absorb the sound is with absorption panels. Absorption panels can be found in many styles but you'll often find them composed of polyurethane foam or fiberglass. They either come as a tile or a brick of foam or as one of the absorptive materials mentioned that is then wrapped in cloth fabric. These are generally several inches thick as the density of the material is important for the absorption and dampening of the sound waves. Now, some people might assume that any sort of foam will do the trick and some do-it-yourself websites suggest using material like a foam mattress topper or the egg crate stuff. However these materials are far too thin, after all it's meant for comfort and is not dense enough to properly absorb sound. Plus generally they will look very ugly.

When placing proper absorption panels around your home studio generally you'll want to situate them at ear level on each wall of the room. These should be at your early reflection points because the monitors should be pointed at your ears to allow you to hear the best audio mix. The sound waves especially the high frequency audio waves will travel out in that direction to your walls and reflect back to your ears causing you to hear the sound waves more than once. By placing absorption panels in these locations you stop that reflection from happening because as the sound that reaches those walls will be absorbed. This helps you to only hear the audio signal as it is coming out of your monitors.

A good way to judge the exact right spot for those absorption pales is with a help from a friend in your home studio. Sit in your chair and have the monitors facing your ears. Have a friend stand against one wall with a mirror and move back and forth along it. Now turn your head or your body towards your friend and follow the mirror. Most likely if you can see the face of the monitor in the mirrors reflection you're going to get an audio reflection in that spot so put some absorption paneling there. Other good places to put absorption panels are the wall directly behind you, the ceiling right above your seat and right behind the monitors themselves. Also having a carpeted floor or placing a throw rug on the floor can help dampen some of those sound waves.

Now you may be thinking, why not use absorption panels over the whole room just to be safe? While that may sound like a good idea in theory that will actually dull the natural acoustics of the room and leave your audio sounding bland. Some say covering about fifty percent of the walls should do the trick however in most home recording studios thirty to forty percent should work just fine. The goal for a home recording studio isn't necessarily a perfect setup it's just improving it as much as you can. Something is better than nothing. However if your budget does allow for fifty percent coverage then go for it.

The other less common option for reducing reflections throughout a home studio is diffusion. Diffusers are mathematically uneven and irregularly shaped surfaces or cabinets with varying depths that allow the audio waves to bounce around and break out without colliding or interfering with each other. This allows the audio waves to scatter so you'd still be able to hear them but with the reduced intensity. That's instead of letting the audio get absorbed. This retains the live ambiance of the sound without an echo. Mostly you will see those in high-end professional studios that can afford them.

Bass Traps

The absorption and diffusion panels will help with those mid and high frequency early reflection. Low end frequencies like those produced from a bass sound can cause their own issues. Luckily there is a solution to that as well. Bass traps, these are generally blocks of foam molded to fit in the corners of a room. They stop low end frequencies from reflecting in those corner areas where they tend to bunch up. Without bass traps there's a high chance of noise cancellation which could make it sound like you are lacking that low end power. Conversely depending on how close you and your monitors are to the corners of your room it could have the opposite effect and sound like you have more bass than you actually do.

Producing Music

It is really easy to start producing your first songs and most DAW's allow you to create a song using mostly software instruments. If you wanted to plug a microphone in or plug in an instrument you can do that too. The realm of creative possibilities are endless.

Before you get started producing music you should remove all creative distractions. Put your phone on silent, turn off the wifi and block off some time. The general atmosphere of a workspace is important. You should want to spend time in there, it should feel comfortable, organization goes a long way. The quicker and better you are, the more time you can spend making music. Learn shortcuts and inner working of whatever you're working with. This will lead to a smooth and seamless workflow

Get inspired and train your musical instincts. Put on your favorite records and analyze the living hell out of them. Listen to each individual instrument. Where is the instrument placed in the soundscape? How loud is it? What kind of effects does it have on it? What kind of feeling does the song evoke? The more you are studying and thinking about this stuff the more you can pick up the elements you like or dislike. You can then add those elements to your music or make sure you avoid them.

When you are producing music, try to focus on the project you're working on and not to work on ten projects at the same time. Because if you're doing the arrangement on one track and then doing it on four or five other tracks when get back to one of them you will kind of forgot where you are. Stick with it and try to finish it in one go. I know it's not always possible. Sometimes you get stuck and you just want to move on. In some cases you can just leave it for a while, let it simmer. Work on something else and then come back with a fresh perspective. Maybe you end up making some huge changes and it becomes a great song. Overall you should aim to finish thing quickly, any mistakes you made can be learned and applied to the next song.

Melody and Chords

There are a number of ways to start a song. Maybe it's a vocal, an idea or a sound. One of the best ways to start a song is with a melody. When it comes to creating the melody, think of a rhythm first and hum it out. You can then record that into your DAW with a midi keyboard or draw it in on the piano roll. It's all about quickly, getting your ideas from your mind and into the computer. Experiment and don't judge yourself.

Once you have your pattern recorded in you want to start thinking about the key of the melody. Find where you want the root note to be. To help you maybe choosing a basic sound at first is a good idea. Test it and listen to where it sounds good. Incidentally at this stage I would usually use a generic piano sound to test out melodies and chords. If it sounds good on there then it will sound good on any other preset. You can always keep moving the arrangement onto the piano to test out the intricacies.

With your root note set you can then start to move the different notes around in the scale. To help you stay within the key scale just draw the notes of the scale into the piano roll of your DAW and then mute them so that you have a visual representation of the key you are working in. Once you have a decent one bar loop melody, start to change it up across the following bars. You want to aim to get a decent four bar loop that has a strong identity throughout. It should be catchy and not overly complex. Listen to The Chainsmokers, Calvin Harris and Dr Dre they all use pretty basic melodies but they are highly effective.

With your melody settled you can now throw down some chords. Record these in if you like or use your music theory knowledge to draw them in. The chords will set the tone and feeling of your loop. Remember to stay in the key of the song. The best way to start with chords is to think about the chord progression in your mind first. What is the rhythm? What is the emotion? You could play the chords in with a midi keyboard or draw them in. I suggest you start with the root notes of the chords. You can then layer some notes over the top to create the chords. This does not necessarily have to be the root note of the key scale. It's all about what you like and what emotions you are trying to convey. Often i like my chords and basslines to be a seventh or fifth below my melody. This creates a really harmonious sound with lots of space and intelligence. For more dancefloor stuff the melodies and chords stay quite basic throughout which allows the song to be more sonically powerful as there is less frequency movement. When you are done, make sure everything is locked in and quantized to the grid.

Bassline

To add to your melody and chords, let's create a bass. Think of how you want your bassline to play and sound. Then either record or draw it in. In most cases your bassline will use the root notes of your chord progression set an octave lower. You could then change up the rhythm a little bit to keep it exciting. Maybe you have an offbeat bass that moves around the kick or maybe your bass is long and slow to come in. Use your imagination and create your vision. The bassline should support the loop and not take away from it.

MIDI and Presets

One of the most difficult things guys for anybody in the creative world is creating a melody and chords. If you show up to the studio and you don't have these ready then your going to struggle. A great and easy way to start a song is with MIDI melodies and chords. Maybe it doesn't feel like the song is yours, however as producers we want to be efficient and instead of wasting hours trying to make a melody, could just use some MIDI. The important thing here is that you have something to start with. MIDI can easily be changed later on and it can then become something more original to you. To find MIDI files just do a quick Google search. You could even find the MIDI of your favorite songs and then try to change or borrow a few ideas.

Other times you might not have any idea or MIDI. In this case what a lot of music producers do is fire up one a VSTI and start scrolling through some presets. Finally you find that one sound and you're like wow I know what to do with this. Boom, the song is done in your head and it's time to get action. To do this you don't need a lot of sound banks or presets, most VSTI's come with great stock plug ins that are equally as good. So go preset scroll guys and hopefully you find a great sound that inspires you to make some music

Beats

Next up you will want to add some drums to support your musical arrangement. Creating good drums is all about choosing the best sounds. You can go in three different directions. Record a full drum set, use loops or create loops with single sampled drum hits. Recording a drum set is quite a complicated task and is only something you would consider if you were working more with live bands. For that purpose you would require a great drummer, awesome microphones and utilization of professional recording techniques. There really are a lot of intricate parts to the process and if you compromise one then the final sound can be really bad.

If your starting out or even at a professional level it is better to use samples. Check out www.splice.com, it is a game changer. For a small subscription paid monthly you get access to a library full of quality samples and presets that you can find listed in various, tags, key and bpm. The service is based on credits so for every download you use a credit and the number of credits you have depends on your payment plan. In addition you can also rent to own some of the leading VST and VSTI's. It really is next level stuff to finding the perfect sounds for your productions. This is great for creating loops or making loops from single, sample drum hits. When it comes to finding the right loop of course you need to have the idea right and then search for the appropriate bpm and feel.

If you decide to start creating beats with individual hits then it will be a highly effective way to create really unique drums that specifically meet the requirements of your songs. The most important part of the process comes in the sample selection. It is like baking a cake, find the right ingredients and you have a great product. Use the rotten ones and it will be bad. What I suggest you do is to start sourcing a few different hits each time and then compare them to find the best. To make it easier you can just load them into your sampler of choice, draw in a pattern in midi and then switch between the different sounds. Decisions should be based on achieving the right pitch, envelope and timbre to gel with your other instruments. Later you can add effects and mixing to gel them together even more.

The main drum elements to build around are usually a kick and snare. The first thing I like to start with is finding a really good kick. It is the foundation of most club music and it really moves you in the club or at a festival. If you select the wrong kick you're kind of already screwed from the start, it would be really hard for you to get anywhere good. If you do find good kick samples you can reuse them on on your tracks. Don't be one of these people that always wants to use something new for the kick, go for the ones where you know that they will work well. The kick should always be in the key of the song, in most cases this would be the root note. Most samples will tell you what the key is but you can also check it out with the stock plugins available in your DAW.

Once you have found a good kick and snare sound you can program in the right pattern for them. Usually that would be quite a simple one and with a drum roll every sixteen bars. Then you can start to fill in the blanks of the frequency spectrum with other drum hits or loops. However this all depends on the music your making, the less melodic it is the more drum elements you usually have so if your melodies are not that interesting and exciting you have to do other things instead. You can fill up the high and high mid frequency range with shakers and hi hats. Or you can also add in some drum breaks to fill up the spectrum nicely. I also like to add some background drum rolls and breaks just as some kind of ear candy. Keep bringing things in and testing them out but make sure they have a purpose and fit the music. It all depends on what kind of music and the vision for it you have.

Tempo

The tempo/ speed of your song is going to have a massive impact on it. You can experiment with different tempos whilst your song is in it's loop stage. Don't get stuck in the box, try out a bunch of different variations. What works really well is to produce a number of variations of your musical elements and melodies before you start to arrange it. You could try it at a really slow tempo with different patterns for your melodies and drums. Or you could go more fast with the tempo and arrange things into a more dance floor structure. Just experiment and go with what you like the most.

To give you some ideas of common tempo's take a look at the following.
Trap and Future Bass - usually around 150 to 155 bpm
Big Room and Progressive EDM - usually around 128 to 130 bpm
Hip Hop - usually around 95 to 105 bpm or 140 to 150 bpm
Tropical House - usually around 100 to 105 bpm
Pop - a lot of pop music is around 100 bpm but there are lot's of variations that incorporate the elements and tempos of other genres such as EDM and Trap.

Arrangement

At this stage you should have a good melody, chord progression, bassline and drums. This will serve as the main part of your song, it's the hook or chorus. Many producers often find it a struggle to turn their loop's into a full song. Don't worry if this happens because you're absolutely not alone, almost all musicians and producers struggle with this. Actually there's loads of practical things you can do to help turn this loop into a song. The first one is all about arranging your song so that it can have structure variety and interest. The second one is about jamming along with the song whether you're by yourself or with friends. You can add creative musical parts as you play along to your song adding things to keep it interesting. The third part is all about how to mix refine and organize your project as you go so that you stay motivated to work on it.

A song is a story that takes the listener on a journey from the start to the end with feelings and emotions. The first step that you can do to get a loop into more of a song format is to actually structure it like a song. There is no standard with this kind of thing but we can look at some of the most common ways to structure a song. Later when you are more experienced you can experiment with different structures. It all depends on what your vision for the song is. Is it aimed at the dancefloor, the radio or for at home listening? If you want to get great at producing tracks start analyzing more music. Pay attention to the arrangements, how do they progress and how do they capture and keep the listeners attention? Famous commercial music producers who are making these smash hits are smart and their songs are constructed so well. I encourage you take an in depth look at some of their music and even spend some of your time trying to reproduce famous songs. Import the whole song and figure out the key, structure, instruments and everything else. If you do that regularly I guarantee you're going to learn some stuff and you can go apply it to whatever else you want to do.

Commercial Music Arrangements

Culturally our ears have been pre-programmed to expect certain things at certain times in music. In commercial music there are four main sections to most songs. A pre chorus, chorus, bridge and verse. A chorus is the main hook of the song and is obviously where you want someone to go to iTunes and click buy. Verses are usually the chill parts of the songs. That's where you're going to tell your story and sort of setup what's to come.The main rule with commercial music is every eight bars you throw something new in because ideally you want to build your songs and carry the listener on a journey.

To start you can begin with a verse or some kind of intro. Normally after a verse we know a choruses is on its way even if it's a pre-chorus we know we're building to a chorus and the listener will expect them to happen at certain times instinctually. After a chorus comes another verse or bridge and if something weird happens it throws people off. By the end of the first chorus you want people to know the song already. When the second chorus comes in you want the listener to already be hooked in and sing it without hesitation so don't change anything, keep the same arrangement. After chorus two you can go to a bridge. At this point the song is as big as it has ever been. It's the most energy that's ever been in the song. A bridge usually happens once in a song and it's sort of your time to get creative like if you want to do some crazy stuff musically there's your spot to do it. Often it is exciting and builds a lot of tension. After that you're usually going to go into another chorus or sometimes depending on the song you can go into another verse but after that it's pretty much like we've hit the peak of the song and we're driving out the chorus. Right then after the bridge we bring things down it's sort of like the calm before the storm the calm before the end of the tune where we just really want to drive it out with the outro which is usually another chorus with some added layers such as more vocals or instruments.

Watch your song lengths overall time. Try to keep it under four minutes, maybe you want to write epic six minute long songs. If your song is seven minutes long it's not going to cut it and you've got to chop it down. Your really not going to see much of anything past five minutes in length.

EDM Music Arrangement

In EDM the structure of a song is a lot more simple because the majority of them are made for the dancefloor and need to be easy for a DJ to mix. The songs are meant to make people dance and are usually three to four minutes long with an intro and outro for DJ to mix in and out of the track and lots of build ups and drops. Typically you will have an intro, build up, drop, break down, drop and then outro. Each section is usually changing every sixteen bars.

The first section would be an intro of sixteen to thirty two bars. A trick I use is to construct this kind of music is to take the main drop part and mute different parts to see what could work as the intro. Or you can take the melody and remove a few notes. Once you figure that out you definitely have made good progress. The intro part should slowly build up as more elements are introduced. This will then go into some kind of breakdown. Usually the drums will stop here and it will be more atmospheric with vocals or some melodies progressing over sixteen to thirty two bars. This will then go into a build up across sixteen bars. This part is really important and you want it to bridge your breakdown into the drop. I suggest you spend awhile on this and test how it sounds transitioning into the drop. You can make some really epic build ups that will make your music highly original and memorable.

Reaching the drop is like your main chorus. It's where your main melody is played along with drums and the full power of your arrangement. This usually last about thirty two bars with some kind of variation in the middle and then a little bit of a different arrangement on the next sixteen bars. Often that is just the addition of a few extra drums, hi hats or extra notes and or variations of the melody. Then the song would breakdown to another atmospheric part that is similar to the first part. A lot of EDM music will use this section to have some kind of synth and chords arrangement for sixteen to thirty two bars here. It's kind of like a bridge where you can show of your musical skills or some really cool sound design. Keep it relevant to the key of the song and perhaps use some new sounds. You can then go back into the build up and another drop. The drop is usually the same as the first one or if your feeling experimental you could try something a little different. Hardwell does this a lot on his second drops as does Dillinja. Listen out for both of them. Finally to finish your EDM song would be the outro which is like the book end and build down of the song. You could then end it with an impact hit, effects or fade out. It's all up to you.

Sound Design

When you have a good vibe going on with your song and the construction is tight the next part is sound design. This is often what takes the longest. Making a unique interesting sound is quite hard especially for synth sounds and is where you can spend a lot of time. This is the main reason why I advise you to separate the sound design from the arrangement part. Of course before you arrange you should have some kind of sound design going on. You can use some basic sounds and presets first off. Then get the arrangement and song idea down fast because sound design can take a long time and you might lose the vibe of the song.

The main reason for sound design being important is because the majority of instrument sounds aren't strong enough on their own. They need more support in order to sound bigger and cut through. Layering and sound design will help to achieve that. The first thing you want to do in this process is decide on that one main sound. Then you can start to add on other layers of sound. The first mistake that a lot of people make is to layer sounds that sound very similar to each other. The perfect example of that is layering supersaws. Yes it's going to sound bigger but you can get the same effect if you were to just compress and put the volume up. So in the case of layering there would be no need to put another synth in the mix.

Layering is all about filling in the areas that are missing in a sound. To help you with decisions, it's a good idea to find a song to reference to. Identify what is missing in your sound versus the reference song. If it's more high end then find a nice bright synth. Or if it lacks a real live feel, then add live instruments and so on. Be objective and purposeful in your decisions.

Another thing to consider is that you make sure you are getting a good balance of mono and stereo. For example, when it comes to layering lead sounds one of your layers should be in mono and then one can take care of the stereo field. This will ensure that the overall sound is mono compatible and it won't get lost in the mix on some mono sound systems.

Finally you want to mix all of your layers into one channel. The benefit of doing that is that now we can compress the individual sounds together. A lot of the time when you layer leads together they will have different dynamic levels. If we glue and compress them together so that they have the same dynamic level it is going to sound more unified. In addition if you want the leads to sound very similar to each other then you can have the same effects on them which would be added to the bus channel. Reverb is great to bring life to the layered sound. There are two ways you can add your reverb. The first way is to add the reverb to a new bus and send the lead signal there or you can just add it to the bus channel. The first option usually creates a better result with a cleaner reverb. To the layered sound I also recommend to add some saturation to gel it together more.

Keep working on your sound design. You can create some really cool sounds but don't get stuck on the details for too long. Focus on finding the right sounds and creating a composite mix of how you imagine it to be. Finally make sure you get it right before you start mixing the song. These are two separate processes and going backwards and forwards between them will waste time and kill the vibe.

Automation

Automation allows us to take any sound and get it to change over time. This will keep the structure and sound design of your songs interesting. You want to keep your listeners locked in. For example you could take a bassline and instead of it coming in really punchy at the beginning you could open up the controls and set it to come in really light. As the intro is happening you could automate this filter to go up or down, whatever you want. Or you could make a sound disappear gradually with the reverb coming up. Most settings on channels, plug ins and instruments can be automated. It is just a case of you simply finding on a parameter and then automating it as you desire. This can be achieved by either recording the movements in or drawing them in by hand onto the particular automation lane.

Reference

Using a reference is a really simple but commonly overlooked method of improving your mixes and productions. You can select a song or a group of songs that you really like for several reasons, including the mixing the mastering, the composition, the arrangement, the sound design or any other factors. It doesn't have to be the most popular music in the world. Simply good music that you aspire towards being able to create or being able to mix in a similar manner. The idea behind this technique is that you can analyze these reference tracks and compare them with the songs you're working on to determine what is lacking or excessive.

A lot of the time when we hear good mixes we're not necessarily in our studio. We might be in the car might or in the gym, who knows where you might be listening. Essentially you need to know what that mix actually sounds like if you were in your studio. Your ears become used to the music you're listening to, so if you're listening to something with a bad mix then your ears have kind of adjusted to the imbalances. If you then listen to a professionally finished mix or one of these reference tracks that you really like it sort of resets what the balance should sound like. You'll immediately be able to hear what you need to change in your song. All of these problems will become really apparent to you. Overall this saves you time if you have something to work towards. If you have something to work towards it's going to save you time because you know what you're aiming towards. Then you can make decisions a lot easier to try and fit your track into that sort of mold. With that being said you're not trying to copy the track. It doesn't matter if your kick drum doesn't sound the same, or your bass doesn't sound the same, or you're using a different snare. That's all completely fine, it's more about the general picture.

Hey, I hope you're enjoying this book….if so please share your feedback with a good review.

Recording

If you want to add in some live instruments or vocals to your songs then it's a great way to make them more original and interesting. Or maybe you are a great guitar player or singer. This will set you miles apart from the majority of producers who are just making music on their laptops. You should always strive to expand on your ideas and more musical minds can create a better song. If you decide to record some instruments or vocals then here are eight tips to help you out.

Recording Tip One

Don't rely on fixing it in the mix. Simply taking the time to get it right in the performance stage will produce much better results. How you play greatly affects your sound. Don't expect to be good right away, practice really does make perfect and there's no magical plug-in or program to make you good. If you want a lot of energy on your recording then you have to record it with a lot of energy. If you want to record quiet then make sure there isn't too much noise or background sound. These kind of performance dynamics can't be achieved with mixing. Never make compromises in the performance stage believing that you can fix it in the mix. It is pretty much impossible to turn a bad recording into a good one. Nine times out of ten its better to go back and record it again.

Recording Tip Two

Use the best microphones, cables and audio interface that you can. Buy the best that you can afford and don't compromise on any of them. Even if you have an expensive interface that won't solve having poor quality microphones and vice versa. Microphone, audio interface and cable choice will greatly affect your sound and it will ultimately make your recordings much better or much worse. Have an idea of what you want. Are you going to do just vocals? Or are you going to be recording an entire drum set? Or are you primarily going to be a guitar player that records the songs at home? Those are very important questions that you need to ask yourself because that will be crucial in figuring out which interface and microphone to buy. These are all equally important parts of the signal. If you cheap out on one then it defeats the point of having one part that is really good.

Recording Tip Three

Know your parts. If you're going to go into a studio and pay a lot of money to be there you should probably know your parts and not figure them out there. Don't waste your money and don't waste the audio engineers time. It will end up being a much better finished product if you are as prepared as possible. Spend the bulk of your time in pre-production. You should be spending significantly more hours preparing your recording than the actual recording itself. Session time is expensive and others people's time is valuable. Do not waste that time fixing something that could've been fixed beforehand.

First and foremost the band, singers or players should be well-rehearsed. The arrangement should be worked out and everyone should know what is expected of them. It's a good idea to record raw demos of your rehearsal. You can analyse them and pinpoint the things you need to work on. You can then also can share them with the producer or engineer so that they know how to prepare for your recording session. If you have a producer on board discuss with them your goals and your inspirations. This will make sure everyone is on the same page and it will help plan out a course of action.

There also a number of small decisions you need to make. Will your recording be done live or will it be multi track overdubbed? Will you be playing with a click? All of these decisions will influence how you prepare. Scheduling should also be done in this pre-production phase. Write up a plan budgeting time for each part of the recording process. Plan on delays and synthesize extra time for creative noodling. Everything will feel better when nobody is stressed out about a clock. This still applies if you are working at your home studio. Try to have as clear a vision as possible and be objective. That way you won't find yourself recording track after track. The more organized and prepared you are the more fun you will have and more fun often leads to good music.

Recording Tip Four
Keep it fresh. This means put new strings on your guitar, new drum heads on your drums. Keep a clean and tidy recording environment. Make sure your singer is not hungover or sick. Be tuned and ready.

Recording Tip Five
Record your vocals clean and isolated. Not everyone has the luxury of an isolation room for recording vocals but if possible try and get into an isolated spot. This could be a closet, a bedroom or just a really quiet small room. I highly recommend a closet with the clothes still in it because that just deadens everything. If you record in a big open room you might get some reverb sound. Also try to avoid being in noisy areas. Having the window open is a bad idea if you live in a city. It is a lot easier to add reverb and sounds than it is to take them out.

Recording Tip Six

Understand the tools. The more knowledge you have of the tools around you, the less of the barrier there is between your musical vision and the end product. Acknowledging music is power. Understanding how your software works, understanding how different microphones works and how it influences sound. Understanding plug-ins, understanding the role of everything in the studio. All these things are highly valuable tools.

Recording Tip Seven

Imagine a soundscape, a visual representation of the instruments playing. This helps organize and arrange the sounds. Ask what kind of feeling am I going for in this recording. For example, if it is a sense of intimacy than use less reverb. Maybe try to make it sound like in a small room. Or for example maybe you want really up front guitars, if so record them close up but be aware of the proximity effect (more on that later).

Recording Tip Eight

Be flexible and take criticism when you're recording. The whole point is for people to hear your music and you better be prepared for criticism because it's going to come whether you are ready for it or not. You should actively seek feedback from the outside. When we are making music we are way into our own heads to be thinking objectively. This outside ear doesn't necessary have to be a musician. After all the untrained ear is going to make up the majority of people who listen to your songs. Ask your family, friends or whoever is around.

How to Record Vocals

There are a lot of variables to recording good vocals. First and foremost you have to be a good singer or have access to one. Because if you're not a good singer then as we already discussed your not going to be able to turn a bad recording into a good one. Again your microphones, cables and audio interface will make a big difference in terms of the sound, so select the best. The room you record in will also massively influence your recording. You probably don't have a whole lot of control over that if you have a home studio. However you can control the distance of your singer from the microphone in addition to microphone placement and how hot you record into your DAW (gain staging). Those factors will make a huge difference in terms of the quality of your vocals.

Another thing that is great for vocals is a pop shield which can be attached to the shock mount. What this does is it kills all the bees, peas and all the natural plosives that are in vocal sounds. When you say those sounds air blasts off your face and overloads the microphone. You probably have heard that sound, it sounds really amateur so don't record any vocals for anything until you have a pop shield. The pop shield will also help force a good distance. Most people record their vocals too close to the microphone and that's a major problem. The singer is just belting away and giving this awesome performance and their mouth is literally an inch or two from the mic. The side effect of being too close is called the proximity effect. When you take a directional microphone such as a cardioid microphone that picks up sounds in one direction. The closer you get to that microphone the greater the base response will be. So if you've ever been using a microphone for singing or speaking then you will notice that if you get really close to it you start to sound a little like Darth Vader because there's that added bump in the bass response. It has no choice but to sound super muddy, there's just no other option. So you record it there and you listen in your headphones while you're recording. Maybe you think yeah this is big, thick and awesome. But later when you go back to mix it you realize there is a lot of unnecessary low end to it. This is pretty much impossible to make sound good. The solution is to just back the microphone away a little bit more. Ideally it should be eight inches to a foot away. What you can do is to take the pop shield and put it about four four five inches away from the microphone. That will be like a boundary which says you can't get any closer and so your vocalist won't get any closer.

The next thing to consider is gain staging and this is so critical. Most people are recording too loud. You really don't need to record things that loud. If you're recording at 24-bit which is what most people are, then you have plenty of headroom and the noise floor is not really an issue. Turn that preamp down, when you're singing or your vocalist is warming up keep your eye on the meter and look at how hot it's getting. Then adjust the volume, the actual gain on that box on your preamp so that you're not peeking anywhere close to the top. You don't want to clip, record so that the meter is around fifty percent of the way up. It will peak a little bit over fiftty percent on some of the loud parts but on average you want to keep it below fifty percent. When you record that low on the meters it looks really unmanly. You feel unmanly and it doesn't look cool to have it way down there. But what matters is, does it sound cool? Because it will sound better when you record it quietly. Not super, super quiet to the point where you can't do anything with it but just fifty percent of the way up is a great starting point. Now if it's not loud enough to you and if you can't hear it or your vocalist is saying turn me up then you don't turn them up on the preamp because you've already got a good level. You turn them up in their mix, it's really easy to set up your headphone sends for their mix and turn that up so they hear what they're hearing. Do not turn up the actual preamp or the audio interface because that's going to affect the actual signal so keep that where you need it.

In conclusion recording good vocals is all about setting the right distance from the microphone, good equipment, acoustics and gain staging. You can apply these principles to recording most instruments also.

Adding Effects and Mixing

Now your at the mixing stage where you can take your song to the next level. It's all about achieving a good balance here. You also need to be objective and productive, don't spend hours here. So many people lose a lot of time here that is completely unnecessary and they end up getting nowhere. If you're feeling overwhelmed by mixing then don't worry because below are fifteen tips to help you succeed.

Mixing Tip One
Before you mix anything make sure it is right at the source. I know you've already heard this but I really can't stress the importance of this enough. Think of it like building a house. If you use bad materials that are decaying and poor quality then no matter how good of a builder you are the end result won't be good. If your recording and mixing, make sure you've got good material. Spend the majority of your time during the recording and production stages. Mixing will be much easier if you put the majority of your efforts there.

Mixing Tip Two

Focus on setting a good volume balance at the start. The foundations of a great mix down come from achieving a good balance of volume at the start and it is paramount to do this properly. Spend the first part of your time on balancing the volume only. Make sure you achieve a great volume balance before you start adding any other plugins or do anything else. Otherwise you will be constantly redressing this during the mixing sessions. You will also need to use volume automation since it is hard to achieve the perfect balance during the whole song. Maybe in some areas the vocals are jumping out or maybe too quiet and automation can adjust that for a particular section.

Mixing Tip Three

Time is essential and mixing sessions should not waste any time. The more time you spend mixing the more difficult it becomes to stay objective. As time progresses you start to lose perspective of what the mix really is sounding like. In addition if your mixing at higher volumes you will also be succumbing to ear fatigue. Make sure you put in time that counts. Prepare your mix before you start. This will allow you to stay objective and be able to mix fast and productively.

Mixing Tip Four

Focus on the main parts. Don't get lost over EQ'ing or compressing some small detail or sound effect in the background. The majority of your mixing should be focused on the mix as a whole picture. Take the stuff that really matters, the vocals, the leads and the main parts. Your priority should be making the stuff that is the listeners focus sound the best. The other elements will follow suit and fit with them.

Mixing Tip Five

Set a loop around the loudest part of your song. When you're doing that preliminary volume balancing it should always be at the chorus or the climax of the song. Mix from this loop because if you use a verse or intro then you can't really build up from that. For example if you had this huge intro then it doesn't leave much room to go from that. The majority of your mixing, adding effects and things should be done at the loudest part. You can always go back to the other sections and add in some volume automation to adjust them if you need to. Your song should really explode into the loudest part with impact.

Mixing Tip Six

Always stay within the big picture. You might think that it is making a difference starting out with EQ,ing and compressing a kick. After all it is one of the most important elements and so you decide to focus loads of time there and then start bringing in other elements. But what you will find is that when you get near the end of the mix, the kick suddenly doesn't work as well. This is because you didn't have it mixed in the context of the mix. Maybe it's conflicting with the frequencies of similar instruments such as the bass synthesizer or maybe it's causing interferences with something similar in the mix. The only way you can really know if you mix it in context with the rest of the mix.

What I strongly suggest is that you begin the mix with the focus on the big picture. Take big broad sweeps and begin with processes like mix buss processing, group processing and the volume balancing. Later on you can zone in on those more intricate details of the mix. Avoid using the solo function of a channel if you can because it takes your sounds out of the context of the mix and then you're probably making the wrong decisions and wasting time. Afterall the listeners won't be listening to anything in solo so try not to use that function, you need to always be in context. If you do struggle with making changes without soloing a channel you can just turn that channel up and make your changes. You will still be in the context of the mix and then you can just drop it back down to where it was. Practice it and develop your hearing.

Mixing Tip Seven

Make sure there is intent behind all of the moves you make. Never do something just because everyone does it or even just for the sake of it. So many producers easily fall into this trap. For example you don't need to apply compression every time, anyway most sounds are already heavily processed. First decide on your intention before taking action. Try to listen with intent and think before you act. Let's say the kick drum is not clear enough, it doesn't stand out and so you apply EQ to emphasize that so that it's really cutting through the mix. But if the kick is already clear in the mix then it doesn't need anymore. Simply leave it as it is. Before making any decision you have to first ask yourself, what am I trying to achieve?

Don't assume you need EQ or compression or effects on every track. The tendency is to slap a plug in on every single track and start fixing or enhancing with the assumption being that every track could be a little bit better with it. Be objective and ask yourself does this track really need any help. If it doesn't and if it sounds good already, then don't put anything on it. The fewer plug is you use the more natural your mix will sound.

Mixing Tip Eight

Analyze your moves. Any time you apply a plugin or change something in the mix, match the volume so that it's the same volume coming out as going in. To be sure you can activate the bypass button to check for volume. Bring it back in with volume and once you've got the same volume turn that bypass button on and off a few times. Does it sound better? Sometimes you might fool yourself so a good thing to do is click it then shut your eyes and turn it on and off many times until you can't remember if it's bypass or engaged. Then you can decide on if it sounds better because then you're really using your ears.

Mixing Tip Nine

Reference your mix against professional songs. This is the process of using a professionally mixed song to check against your mix so you can hear where you're going wrong what you might need to do. Don't use one, try three or four because then you get a better range of reference material. Use a few in a similar genre and in the same key because the bass will change in volume when key changes. It could even be songs that you've mixed in the past that you really like or they could be from up-and-coming artists and mixing engineers. It's just anything that really inspires you and the mixing that you really enjoy.

So if you download the song and you pull it into your DAW you can just put it on its own track and compare it to your song. Pay close attention to specific of the mix against your mix. Low pass and listen to the low end. Does your mix have too many low frequencies or are there not enough? Analyze the top end, is there too much or not enough? How loud should the drums be? How loud is the vocal? Am i using too much reverb?

A lot of people will compare and find the finished track will be a lot louder because it's mastered. This can be really demotivating to compare your rough mix to a completely finished and professional product. So you need to start by level matching and just taking the volume down until it matches the rough volume of your track. Get used to the overall balance, mute it and then unmute your song and take a listen to it and just try to listen for overall differences. Use your ears you'll be able to hear pretty big differences and start honing in on problems in your own mix. But if you're not quite trusting your ears there's a few tools that you can use to help you out. The tonal balance tool from iZotope is pretty handy and this sort of breaks down the frequency spectrum into bands and shows you the distribution of frequencies, much like a spectrum analyzer. It can show you whether you have too much bass or too much high end compared to the references. Or you can listen to the reference track through that and see sort of what their curve looks like and then compare it to the curve or spectrum of your own song. You can see whether there's any peaks or troughs that don't really add up to see whether there's anything missing. As usual it's always best to trust your ears but sometimes having these extra visual tools can help you when mixing. But remember that it really does come down to your ears so just because a tool says that you're in the right tonal balance it doesn't necessarily mean it's right for your song. If you're not using references already then start doing this right away because it will massively improve your mixes.

Mixing Tip Ten

Most of your mixing should be done in mono. This will help you to create separation between sounds by using simple volume balancing, equalization and volume automation. Working in mono will push you to really get the best results between sounds. For example you must make sure there is nothing sticking through or clashing with each other. There should be clear separation and this has to be done primarily with setting volume and EQ. Once your near the final stages of the mix that's where it's okay to start panning and applying stereo effects. Then it will open out the mix because it will already sound very clear and separate. Stereo effects and panning will then make it even better. Most DAW's come with a mono feature or plug-in that you can apply to the master output and turn it off and on to go from stereo to mono.

Mixing Tip Eleven

Listen to your mix on various sets of speakers, sound systems and headphones. During the mixing process, this is an easy way to refresh your ears and perspective whilst checking how your mix translates across different systems. You can test it out on your pocket headphones, mixing headphones, your monitors, computer speakers, club PA, car stereo and anything else you have access to. It will sound different on each and your aim should be to strike a nice balance between all of those. Maybe that means some compromises on one system but for the better of them all. Testing it on the different systems and then going back to the mix to make adjustments will give you a well balanced mix. In addition it will also to reset your ears and give you a fresh perspective on the mix. Incidentally to gain more perspective and be consistent it's really important to take regular breaks, maybe every hour or so.

Mixing Tip Twelve

Mix at low levels. Many people mix way too loud and that is bad for your hearing and also decisions. When we turn things up too loud it often gives us an incorrect perception of frequencies. Ideally you should be mixing around the average level of conversations. If someone at the other side of the room can hear you speak when your mixing then your speakers are set at a good level. Or if you can clearly hear yourself speak, again the speakers are probably set at a good level. Going louder than that would be too much. However for example, sometimes you might want to go loud so you can really hear the low frequencies or sometimes you might want to turn it down so you can focus more on the vocals. In those cases you can use the volume knob as a tool but in the majority of cases you should be at conversational level.

Mixing Tip Thirteen

Take breaks often. We've already talked about this a little, but make sure you take regular breaks. Every hour or so is a good idea. Those breaks will help to reduce ear fatigue and give you a fresh perspective on the mix. Overall it will help you to maintain objectivity. On a macro level if your mixing day in day out you should try to take off a day every week or over longer periods maybe a week or more. Mixing can be very subjective and you can get buried in it. Sometimes you just need to step back and see what your doing.

Mixing Tip Fourteen

Never underestimate the power of volume automation. You can never achieve the perfect balance without using some volume automation. Each section of a song is different and the instruments will behave differently. For example at some sections the vocals become too quiet or there is a solo guitar section that you want to turn up in the chorus to increase the impact. Volume automation is a really powerful technique in this regard. It is extremely likely that the song will require some volume automation to maintain a decent balance during the whole of the song. But don't worry you don't you have to go and automate every channel, remember to be purposeful and listen to what is going on through the different song sections. Listen for things that suddenly start sticking out or that become too low. Volume automation is easy and can be done at the end in a few minutes.

Mixing Tip Fifteen

You don't need expensive plugins and you don't need to buy any extra plugins to achieve a great mix. Almost every DAW comes with good stock plugins and they keep on improving. Take responsibility and stop blaming your plugins if your not happy with your mixes. You can upgrade and start thinking about premium plugins when your mixes are sounding awesome using only stock plugins. Then it will just be about getting that final extra bit of quality with some new plugins. Try and keep it to a minimum, be minimalistic about plugins and have a go-to plug in for for every type of process. Have a go to EQ, a go to compressor, etc. You don't need to spend a fortune either. There are really good quality, affordable plugins out there, just take a look at the previous chapters.

Mixing Tip Sixteen

Be careful when using presets on your plug ins, they might seem magical and easy. For example, let's say you are working on the EQ of a male vocal and you load up a preset that says male vocal EQ. Why not, it makes total sense? However, what this does is it applies a specific EQ curve that the plug-in developers have decided is a good EQ curve for a male vocal. The problem with that is they have no idea what your vocal sounds like. In fact every preset would run into similar issues. They also have no idea of how it correlates within the mix. Essentially what they are doing is making suggestions of typical boosts and cuts on a male vocal. This makes sense in one regard because as you mix more you will stumble across some patterns and some go to starting points. But every vocal is different and this also applies to any other sound. Use them as a starting point but make sure they do what you want.

In addition, don't rely on visual references. If you find yourself making changes because you'd like to see a certain bump there or a certain cut there then you might be making mistakes. There have been so many studies done which prove our hearing is actually impaired by visual stimuli. In fact there is more brain activity when our eyes are closed listening to a piece of music than when our eyes are open. So actually looking at the screen while you mix can be dangerous. Use the bypass button, close your eyes and turn it on and off, on and off and see if it really is helping.

Now, lets take a look at some of the main tools we can use in mixing.

Compression

Compression is a tool that we use all the time in mixing. It controls volume and turns things down when they get too loud whilst turning up the quiet parts. Essentially it reduces the dynamic range of a sound. For example if someone talks loudly and quietly, a compressor will bring the levels closer to the same volume which makes it easier to hear.

Every compressor can be a little bit different but generally they will have the following components. Threshold, this determines when compression starts happening. If you pull the threshold down more compression happens and you can see that by the meter which will be showing the gain reduction. It will be telling you by how many decibels the compressor is turning the signal down. To set it just pull it down until some compression starts happening. On some compressors there is a knee control which sets the angle of compression. You can make it smooth for a gradual turning on of the compressor or more sharp for instant compression. Once the signal crosses the threshold the question is how much is it going to turn it down. Is it going to turn it down a little bit or a lot a bit? The parameter that determines is the ratio. The more we turn this up the more the signal gets compressed. Generally you should stick in the 2 to 1 and 4 to 1 ratio range and then occasionally go up higher if you need to have more aggressive compression.

Next up are gain controls. After the signal is compressed we need to use make up gain to get the volume back to where it was before compression so that we're hearing it at roughly the same volume. This allows us to hear really what's happening. If all we're hearing is volume difference we will think the louder one always sounds better. The whole reason we use compression and the only way to hear that is to make sure we've done some level matching before and after. Some compressors feature an input meter and also output meter which allows you to visually match things up. In addition some compressors have an auto gain button that will do that for you. sometimes they work well and sometimes they don't. In most cases it's more accurate and preferable to manually adjust.

The final two knobs that we need to pay attention to are attack and release. This has to do with how quickly the compressor turns the signal down once it crosses the threshold. Does it turn it down immediately or does it let some of the signal through and then turn it down? What determines that is the attack setting. This is one of the most important settings you can use when compressing. If you go really fast on the attack then it's going to clamp down on that signal really fast and it won't let much of a transient through. Sometimes that's exactly what you want and sometimes it's not. Personally I like to leave some attack time in there so that that punch can come through. Fast attack times can work well on things like vocals but I prefer slower attack times, usually on things like a drum buss or a snare drum by itself can be really cool with a fast attack.

If attack has to do with how quickly the compressor clamps down then release has to do with how quickly the compressor let's go of the sound. The faster we release the more we will hear the stuff that happens after. The longer we make the release the more the compressor will hold down on that signal and it will end up being kind of a quieter tone because we're not letting a lot of the in-between sounds come through. A lot of compressors will have an auto/adaptive button to set the release according to the signal. Again you can experiment manually versus auto.

Multi Band Compression

Multi brand compression is exactly the same as standard compression but with the ability to compress frequencies in four different frequency bands. Essentially it gives you four compressors for every band. They are low (about 0 to 150

Hertz), low mid (about 500 to 5 kilohertz) high mid (about 5 up to 15 KHZ and then high (about 15 up to 20 KHZ). Every multiband compressor r allows you to change these points and can compress every frequency range with a different setting. You can use multi-bang compression for example to just compress the low-end of a mix or maybe to squeeze the mid-range of a drum loop. It is a really helpful tool for shaping sounds and giving them a nice compressed, together sound without over compressing the whole frequency spectrum. Sometimes the low end might be fine and you just want to tame the high end a little bit.

Equalization (EQ)

EQ is an essential tool in mixing your projects. It is a very powerful way of processing sounds and making them fit in the mix. Essentially you can use it to either cut or boost a sound at a certain frequency range. It can help remove or reduce unwanted or resonant frequencies. Or it can turn up the ones that you want. It can be used to help clear up your mix by preventing different sounds from clashing in the same frequency band. When used in conjunction with compression it is a very powerful way of processing your sounds to your liking.

Every single sound that you hear is made up of frequencies. Different types of sounds and instruments tend to live in certain regions on the frequency spectrum. For example drum sounds such as high hats or claps reside in the treble and high mid regions. Leads, pads, vocals, guitars and stuff like that tend to reside in the mid to high mid regions. Whilst sounds like bass lines and kick drums tend to predominantly reside down in the sub and bass regions. Ultimately of course all these sounds can bleed over into the surrounding regions.

Equalizers have a number of bands that serve as control points along the frequency spectrum to let you manipulate sound. Each of these bands have properties associated with them. These properties are the frequency or where along the frequency spectrum you want the sound to be adjusted. Amount, which is set in decibels. A positive number means you're boosting and a negative number means you're cutting. The next property is shape or type. By default equaliser bands are usually set as a peaking type which looks like a bell curve type of shape. A bandwidths resonance or Q determines how wide or narrow the curve affecting the sound is. A much narrower band and will affect only a certain limited number of frequencies whilst a much wider band will affect a lot more surrounding frequencies. Narrow bands can be good for removing narrow resonant frequencies which sound bad. Wide bands can be used for a smooth boost in a region.

Another shape you can set is to use shelving. A low shelf would smoothly turn up or down low frequencies whilst a high self would do the same but to high frequencies. Then there are a high pass and low pass shape which basically states that any frequencies above or below where the band is set are allowed to pass. The difference from a high pass and a low shelf is that a low shelf goes down and then stays at a certain value whilst a high pass cuts off completely at a certain value.

Using an EQ is similar to how it's done in a compressor, it all depends on what you're trying to accomplish or what sound you're going for. Every single sound has its own special requirements. There's really no way that I or anyone else can tell you how to equalize every single sound so what I recommend you do is you get comfortable with EQ. Get good at using the tools and the techniques and before you know it EQ will become second nature to you.

De-esser

A de-esser is used to remove sibilant sounds from an audio recording. In most cases this comes from the really dominant S, F, T or Z sounds produced by vocals. These can really stick out and can be really sharp. The sharpness of these sounds is really determined by the microphone that you are using and the amount of compression that you apply to your recording. If you apply a lot of compression to your vocal recording these sounds can get a lot sharper. Also applying EQ in the high frequencies could make these sibilant sounds even more sharp.

The frequency of sibilant sounds is affected by the vocalist. Most de-esser plug-ins will let you choose between male or female settings and they even let you choose a frequency band. Essentially what it will do is it to reduce the sibealence by applying compression to that frequency group. In essence it is like a multi-band compressor but on the high frequencies only. When adding it to the signal chain if we're going to use a compressor and a de-esser it's best to use the de-esser before the compressor because compression will make the sibilant sounds even sharper. If we put a de-esser behind our compressor it has to work a lot harder so the best thing is to put your de-esser before the compressor so we actually already try to smooth out these sounds before we actually compress a vocal.

Reverb and Delay

Have you ever sang in the shower and felt like you should be singing on stage in front of thousands of people? Well that is because the bathroom is full of reverberation. In fact this used to be a common way to record singers and certain instruments. Stick them in a bathroom or any room with lots of reverberation and when you record them the microphone will pick up all the natural reverb of the room. These days we tend to record in dry rooms and apply a digital reverb or delay afterwards to create a sense of natural ambience and space.

Reverb is created when a sound is reflected from the surfaces or the objects around you. Walls, furniture and hard surfaces all cause a build-up of sound reflections to which then decay. Although you don't have to be in an actual room to create reverb effects you can also create artificial reverbs using plug ins. It is probably the most popular effect used in music but like with any effect if you use it too much you can end up spoiling a good sound. Reverb is mostly used to give a sense of realism to your sounds or you can go crazy and create wild and original sounds with huge depth. For example if your vocals were recorded in an isolation booth then they might sound a little bit dry. You can add reverb to liven them up. You can also use reverb to create space and push things back in the mix, normally with more reverb things will sound like they are further back. The best way to apply reverb is using a send and return. Simply you can put a reverb on a mix bus channel and then slowly send your signal to that channel. This will give you much more control and will sound a lot cleaner.

Many times either instead of or in combination with reverb we also use something called delay. Reverb and delay both create echo an effect. With delay you can create timed very specific echoes whereas with reverb the echoes build up in a more random way. As with reverb you can control the delay effect in many different ways. You can take the same single echo and make it happen many times or even make the delay echoes repeat at different times on the left and right stereo field. Sometimes we use delay instead of reverb but many times we use both.

Limiter

A limiter is something that is so commonly misunderstood and really horribly misused on in mixing, especially by beginners. In basic terms a limiter is just a really extreme compressor. Now a compressor as you may remember is something that we use to control the dynamic range or the difference in volume of a recording. The way you do that is you set a threshold and if the volume goes over that threshold it is reduced a little bit by a ratio that you set. This allows you to control the loud parts and then you apply makeup gain or a little bit of extra volume to get the quieter parts up to the same level. A limiter applies the same concept except when the volume hits the threshold it can't pass any further.

Limiters are usually used at the stage of mastering and that stage comes when you've mixed all the elements in your song. When using a limiter you've got two main aims and that's to raise the overall volume of the sound and secondly to stop loud peaks from coming through. The limiter has a threshold of zero dB and when the volume goes above that it's simply not allowed to pass above. You can apply a limiter so that you can turn the volume of your sound up without causing it to clip. This works great on squeezing together drums. Just be careful not to push it too hard and cause distortion, unless that is what you want.

Saturation

If you have been making music or mixing for a while then you've probably come across the term saturation. There are loads of different types of saturation and they all have their own special qualities and characteristics. Saturation types are often emulated on analog recording devices or mediums such as tape or preamps that are driven too loud. Unlike digital distortion or digital clipping where it hits zero and then it just starts cracking which sounds terrible, usually the way that audio breaks up in the analog domain sounds really nice and pleasing. All of these distortions and characteristics are all due to the imperfection of that recording medium but it just so happens to be that those imperfections actually sound really good to the human ear. Some people say it creates a warm sound. Experiment with lots of different types of saturation, it can really enhance your sound even if you're only using a small amount. Overall let your ears guide you and if you like the sound of it then that's the right one for you.

Chorus and Flange

The chorus effect is essentially duplicating a sound but slightly detuning it at the same time. In addition it also pans the sounds. Depending on your preference you can adjust all of these parameters to make the effect be more fast or slow. This is great way of adding warmth and depth to your sounds. It can turn plain narrow sounds into thick harmonies. Flange is similar but a little bit more extreme and is used more as an ear candy kind of effect. Be careful when applying it to bass instruments as it doesn't work too well in the lower frequencies.

Auto tune

You're probably already familiar with Auto-Tune, or rather, pitch correction. For most people "Auto-Tune" has become synonymous for all kinds vocal processing. But actually, the branded processor Auto-Tune can only do a specific set of things. The first hit single to use Auto-Tune was Cher's "Believe," and it used the most extreme setting, making it sound robotic in a way. That kind of sound had not been heard before, so within a year of the release of "Believe," Auto-Tune had been sold to every major studio in the world. The inventor said that Auto-Tune might be to music what Photoshop is to photography: everyone uses it, but not many are keen to admit it.

Basically, Auto-Tune takes the incoming signal, that is, the voice, and takes it to the closest note, making it in pitch. You can think of it sort of like a guitar where wherever you push on the neck, you'll get a real note because of the frets, but the voice without Auto-Tune is more like a violin, where you have to kind of slide around sometimes to get to the note you want. The pitch of a note is defined by its frequency, and this is measured in Hertz. The note A has a frequency of about 440 Hz while the closest note above it, A sharp, has a frequency of about 466. So if I would sing a note in between these two frequencies, Auto-Tune would try to correct it either to A sharp or to A. But changing the frequency is only part of what Auto-Tune does. Have you ever wondered why speeding up a song sounds like a chipmunk is singing? It's because you are increasing the frequency of the sound. But it also means you're shortening the note. So the cool thing that Auto-Tune does is that it changes the frequency and the length of the note.

There are a few positive things that modern vocal production has allowed for in music. First off, more precise vocal recordings. Secondly, it has allowed for faster work flows in the studio meaning that your favourite artists can make music way faster. So even though your favourite artist probably "cheats" a bit in the studio, try to remember that the tracks that you love by them might not have existed without this technology speeding up their workflow.

Mid Side

Mid/side processing has to do with the way phase works and sound is captured. Imagine that whatever comes from the center in other words mono means that it's being played at the same time on both speakers. Then there is everything else, whatever is played by the speaker's not at the same time that is going to be the difference. When you use Mid Side techniques instead of having left and right you have sum and difference. If for example increase the side part of the effect then your mix will be a lot wider. You could for example brighten up the side information and that will result in the top end being brighter but just in the stereo perception of the sound. Conversely you can decide for example to make the vocals louder just by pushing the mid of the side information. Or you may also decide to increase the low and just of whatever is mono in your mix.

There are many EQs available that have mid side capability, including stock plug-ins. Experiment with them and see what sounds best, find what works for you. Always make sure that you double check by pressing the mono button on your monitor so that you do not create any problems with the phase. You may choose to use mid/side compression, for example if you have backing vocals so you can decide to have a different behavior for compression on the sides or on the mono information that will change slightly the relationship of the backing vocals and the lead vocals within your mix. With all these techniques be very careful because you can change the sound quite dramatically. You should always bypass to check.

Analyzer

Spectrum analyzers give you a graphical representation of what's happening in the frequency range. In essence a spectrum analyzer allows us to see graphically what's happening within the frequency range. Many DAWs nowadays come with a spectral analysis built into every single individual track so you can use those. This is important because many of us being bedroom producers or having home studio setups don't have the greatest sounding rooms. Unless you have an acoustically treated studio space you know you're kind of at the mercy of you know your room.

What you might want to consider doing if you're going to start using a spectrum analyzer is to find a song that you think sounds amazing and use it as a reference. Look at the frequency curve of it compared to yours. If the frequency analysis doesn't look like the reference, no matter what you think it sounds like then your ears are deceiving you because the sound is bouncing around the room. You will be totally getting a distorted representation of what's going on.

An example of it's application could be to check the bump on the kick. Maybe you should have more of a bump and maybe turn up the kick or add some EQ at a specific frequency. Maybe you should raise the high hats or some of the upper register instruments. Use the analyzer as a visual guide and just really study the curve. Where are the bumps, where is it straight, where does it roll off? Use your eyes to help your ears and what you're going to find is as long as your curve matches their curve is that you've got a balanced mix.

In addition there are also analyzers for stereo width. Again you can check against a reference track to make sure your song is the right width. Typically you would do check across four frequency bands. Low, low mid, high mid and high. Most songs gradually widen from the low to the high. You can set those accordingly.

Side Chaining

Side chaining is a useful tool for allowing instruments at similar frequencies to fit together in the mix. The most common use of it is with a kick drum and bass line. Having a clear kick in dance music is really important and it can often get buried in the mix. There are two ways to use sidechaining. The first is with an LFO tool and the second using mix sends. If you use an LFO tool you would simply apply this to your bassline and set it's speed to fit with the pattern of the kick drum. The goal is that the lfo tool causes the bassline to drop in volume whenever the kick hits. You can adjust the envelope to suit this. I recommend you print your bassline and then import it back in as an audio file to ensure the ducking is correctly lined up.

The second way to apply sidechaining is a little bit more complicated. You need to use a compressor with the side chain facility available. Most of the big name DAW's will have a stock plug in featuring this. Next you need to insert the compressor onto the bassline channel. You would then select the input source to be whatever channel the kick is on. The signal from that will now be sent to the compressor causing to duck the volume of the bassline whenever the kick hits. This is great for other genres that don't use the standard 4/4 pattern of dance music. Since the lfo tool is more suited for that. You can then adjust the compressor attack and threshold to set how quickly and how much the compressor alters the bassline volume.

Be Minimal

A word of warning, you should be using as few plugins as possible. The reality is w we have access to so many great sounding plugins and we feel the urge to use so many. You can go crazy with effects and have as many versions of them inserted in your tracks as long as your computer can handle it. The temptation is to cover up our weak recordings with tons and tons of processing in hopes of turning it into something amazing. We shouldn't have to use so many plugins. Use as few plugins as possible. Technically speaking the more plugins you add the more processing and math your computer's having to do. More math means it's having to think harder and that affects the actual audio processing. In turn it doesn't keep the quality or the fidelity of the audio as pristine as it could be. The psychological benefit of using as few plugins as possible is it stops you in your tracks. It makes you ask yourself, what is this going to accomplish, what is the purpose of this plug-in? It forces you to have a reason for the mixing decisions you make which is so valuable. Work with great recordings and you will only need to do as little as possible. Don't harm your audio you don't over process it. Think strategically about what do you need to do and then you grab those tools and you use them.

Mastering

Mastering is the final process of enhancements and tweaks that we make to a song before it gets released or sent out. When you are happy with the mix and production it's time to get your song sounding big, fat, full and loud. You will want it to be just as good as all the other commercial stuff out there. There are many different ways to master and I'm just going to show you the way that I figured out over the years that's gotten me the most consistent results. Don't focus too much on the exact software or plugins, you can get great results with any program and any decent plugins. What I really want you to get is the principles. These can be explained in three stages, preparation, enhancement and checking.

When you are mastering remember that your ears get tired so you don't listen for hours and hours on end. Take regular breaks, every hour or son. In addition try and listen at a low volume for the majority of the time. At some times you might want to go loud in order to hear the bass and low frequencies. But don't get stuck there.

Preparation Stage

The first stage is to check through the track and make sure it is free from defects or sound artifacts. Make sure there's no noise and make sure there's no kind of clicks or pops. Before you even think about mastering it's really important to make sure it sounds the best it can be. Otherwise you will keep going back to the production and mixing stages. No matter how much you try and fix a bad recording or bad mix is still going to end up bad. Ideally you don't to go back to the mix phase or the recording phase but inevitably there might be things that you have to fix and at least you need to watch out for. Look out for obvious things like excess noise, especially in the beginnings and the ends or on the quiet parts things. Also different frequencies may be jumping out such as a certain bass note jumping out of the mix. Pay attention for those things because if possible it's better to go back to the mix fix.

Before you send out your final mix to be mastered, drop your input. When you are exporting your mix you want to aim for around minus 6 dB of headroom because you will need some room to play with. The headroom will allow you space to use your mastering tools. Next, set up you project. I recommend you import two or three reference tracks. These should be in the same key and have a sound that you would like your final master to be like. When you analyze your references against your song, the reference will look a lot fatter and bigger. That's what we are trying to get our song like. First what we're going to do is we're going to try and chop off any peaks and squash the whole thing down to get it to looking like the reference but more importantly sounding like it.

Enhancement Stage

The next stage is enhancement and this is just anything that makes the track sound better. It might be EQ tweaks, some exciters, bass boosts or dynamics processing, etc. If you are working on an album, it should fit in the context of a whole album. You want the tracks to flow from one to the next and so you don't want this really loud song next to a really quiet song.

Now in this phase there are a lot of things we can do to make it sound better. Maybe clean it up a bit or maybe just add a bit of something to it. For example maybe fatten it up a bit with low end boosters or add a bit of EQ on the top-end to brighten it. The first plugin I use would be just a standard EQ set up with a high-pass filter. All this is doing is just taking out all the frequencies below a certain point. You can set it really low at 40 Hertz and with a standard slope. This is just to clean up any potential low-end rumble. Since there's nothing down there that's that useful you can just cut it and allow more space in the mix. Low frequencies tend to take up the most space soe remove the ones that cannot be heard.

The next thing I would add is some valve or tube emulation. This will fatten up the mix a little bit and add some low-end meat. You can also add a tape emulator which will also add some bottom end and subtle saturation to the mix. Experiment with both, on some songs they will work and others maybe not. If your mix is still lacking low end you can use a great plug-in from Waves, called max base. What it does is to emulate and add frequencies in the low to low mid range. This is going to make the song sound fatter on smaller systems like iPod headphones, laptops and things like that. If you're doing music like hip-hop or trap it is an amazing plugin because often we lose fatness in a track. Because these saturation effects often take off some of the top end and makes it sound a little bit dull you will want to add a little bit of an EQ. Use this to add some sheen on the top end, but in a subtle way. Don't overdo it and make sure you check against your references. Also, always bypass to compare the dry origin. The EQ you use should be a very transparent.

Next you will want to add a little bit of compression to glue the track together. You should use it sparingly. You literally want like one or two decibels of gain reduction at the most. It should be just touching it to glue the track together a little bit more.

You can use a multiband compressor to actually solo each frequency because for example you may not want to compress the mid-range which is the most obvious part of the mix like where the vocals are. You don't want to compress that as much because it will result in sounding overly compressed. However you probably want to compress the low end and bass so that it sounds really fat without disappearing. Overall you want to set a threshold at the level that they are peaking at and then adjust the gain make-up to make it a lot clearer and just bring it all together.

The next thing I want to add is a stereo widener. I would suggest using a multi-band stereo widener so you that can set each band to be at different widths. Check against your reference tracks to hear how wide or narrow each band is. Should it be wider in the high, is it to narrow? Is the low end too wide? You can look at the reference screen and make adjustments accordingly. Most mixes will tend to be more narrow at the bottom and then widen towards the top. When you narrow bands be careful that it doesn't cause sounds to cancel eachother out. Always check before and after.

Next comes the clipping stage. what we're going to do here is chop off any peaks in order to get the mix more squashed and fat. However we don't want to distort the sound by pushing it too far because that will not sound good. We we want to use something that clips the signal but also sounds good and this is actually one of the secrets that the mastering professionals use to get songs really loud. They are actually driving them through these really expensive converters. Now you probably dont have really expensive converters. But you can use a decent saturation or clipper plug in to slowly saturate the track and chop the peaks off. Start playing the track and slowly push it until you hit the sweet spot. After that bring down the output to leave room for the limiter which we will add in the next phase.

The limiter is the last plug-in that you will use. This is the most essential plug in and what this does is to set the final output ceiling. The standard is to set it to minus 0.1 which means that it's not going to let any sounds go past minus 0.1. Zero is clipping so we are going just below that to avoid any clipping. Then as we drop the threshold of the limiter it'll start to limit and squeeze the sound more. We can also use a multiband limiter if we prefer so that it's actually limiting each band.

When it comes to setting the final volume it's a case of preference and reference. Compare to some of these other masters just to see where you are in terms of volume. You can use the metering function of the mixer to get an average level of the song you are referencing against. Remember to always bypass any effects so you can hear what they are doing and if they are working as you want. If your mix is sounding louder or quieter than your reference record then you're probably doing something wrong. Usually it has to do with the low end because it's easy to get a song loud and sort of like harsh signing but to get it loud and fat that is the challenge. So if you need to go, go back and adjust your signal chain until you get your master how you want it.

<u>Checking Stages</u>

The final step is to export the mix and test it on a whole bunch of different systems. Try it on a small radio, headphones, in the car on something with a subwoofer or in the club, wherever you can. The goal is so that you can hear what that sounds like on the different systems. However don't make final decisions based on one system but if you notice that say on like four different systems the bass is too high or it's sounding too thin on all the different systems then it probably will need those adjustments. If you can strike a great balance on all the systems then you have a winning mix.

Finally then comes the formatting and this just involves all the admin things like naming the tracks putting in some kind of codes in case you want the names to come up and the album cover to come up in some media players. It is also the final format stage that you're saving this whole thing to. Is it going to CD or is it going to MP3? For CD quality settings you will need to export at 44.1 kHZ with bit rate of 16 bit. For MP3 you will need to export at 320 kbps with a bit rate of 16 bit.

Hey, I hope you're enjoying this book....if so please share your feedback with a good review.

Conclusion / Finding Your Sound

Your sound isn't something you discover once and for all in fact it's something you develop. So if you're sitting down to produce or write just one song, instead of sitting around and trying to discover what that sound will be before you do anything you might want to just start with the rough idea of the song. How are you going to know what your sound is before you even start making music? It it just doesn't make sense, it's like having an author say I want to be an author and I want to know what my writing style is in my voice without ever writing anything. To be an author you have develop your own voice and write more books. The same is true for you as a musician and an artist, you have to record songs, write songs or release songs to develop your sound as an artist. Now imagine that over a course of an album. Imagine that over the course of a career as an artist. It is the long term process of making music and putting it out there that will develop your sound. Laying down a simple track or creating a drum loop won't develop your sound.

Think about your favorite bands or artists, they all have a distinct sound. When you're sitting down to write music and create music you should always be developing you sound. Everyone has to figure out their own unique sound. A common mistake people make here is that they can't sound like anybody else. That's kind of an arrogant position. There are very few people who are original and even those people aren't truly original because we have all been influenced by someone else. Your goal shouldn't be to sound totally unique and unlike anyone else because in doing that you start from a negative place of I don't want to sound like them. Come at it from a positive place which is who do I sound like or what do I want to sound like. The difference is huge because you can create and discover your sound when you're looking for what you want as opposed to saying this is what I'm not.

Let yourself intentionally be influenced by other artists. Look at artists or bands or records or specific songs that you want to listen to and intentionally try to be influenced by them. Now this is different than copying. For example, Daft Punk specifically wanted to recreate that seventies funk and soul sound on their last record and so they specifically listened to records from that era. They were heavily influenced intentionally because they wanted to kind of recreate that sound but what came out of that was a grammy award winning, completely original sounding record. Listen to a wide range of music, not just new music but older records too. You can develop and still sound fresh by borrowing ideas from decades ago. Let those influences come together and mash them into this incredible new sound. If you want to make great music you need to listen and obsess over great music all the time. Everybody is influenced, the only reason you know about music is because you've heard it. The only reason you know how to play guitar or piano or drums or whatever is because you've heard other people play. You are so influenced by other people, it's unavoidable and that is okay. The more you listen to great music the more ideas start popping in your mind and you actually can create faster.

The Power is in The People

Collaborate with other people, you can discover something new in yourself that you never would have done before. Having a network of other musicians, producers, engineers and people in the music space around you is probably the most important thing to developing your sound and becoming successful. Big opportunities often come from connecting with people, reaching out to people, jamming with people and taking calls with people. They don't necessarily have to be in your preferred genre. Ask any major producer or musician and they would say the same that their biggest opportunities came from connecting with other people and having a network.

Find music related events in your area and go to them.This could be events like on meetup.com or music expos or open mic nights anything that's music related that's happening in your area period go to it. If there's nothing in your area, go to another area where there is something happening. Check classified ads in your local paper or craigslist ads for engineers or musicians or mixers who are trying to get hired for certain gigs in your area and contact them. Not to hire them but just to tell them that you admire their work like. Say hey I just saw your ad on Craigslist or whatever you're super talented I love your work I'm not trying to hire you necessarily I'd love to just meet up for coffee man and just talk music with you and maybe we can encourage each other. Reach out to people you admire and offer anything you can think of for them and don't expect anything in return. Think about how you can add value to their life in any way. Generally people will give back and a lot of times what happens when you serve somebody like this they give to you without them realizing it. Your next big opportunity may not even come from the person you reached out to or the person you gave to but they will in turn pass your name along to somebody else.

No Excuses

Get out there and actually make some killer music. If you have good ideas, talent and a drive to make music then there are no more excuses to not make music. There used to be excuses. It used to be that equipment was expensive, the studios were hard-to-find but those excuses are out of the window. Most people will say I don't have the right equipment or the right room and a blah blah blah. Newsflash none of that matters, the gear you use does not matter that much. You can start with your affordable equipment and keep it and just use what you have and get better at it. Technical stuff will only get you so far even though that's what we think we need. But none of that will make any difference unless you have the correct mindset. That isn't just fluff, it's not motivational stuff but stuff that actually helps you achieve tangible results aka creating and releasing great sounding music.

Maybe what also holds you back is the common feeling that we never feel like we're good enough and there's always more to learn. You got to get over your fears and actually release some music. Realize you're not going to be amazing the first time you release something. Yes, there are some key things you do need to know to get really good sounding recordings with your gear but it's a lot easier than you think.

Maybe you never have the time. Your busy with a job, married and got kids. Music isn't going to be the most pressing thing in your life and so it gets pushed to the back. It gets pushed to the late nights, it gets pushed to the weekends, it gets pushed to next month which becomes next year and finally becomes never. But there are ways to better leverage your time so that you can do all the things you need to do and still have time for the things that you really want to do. You can always find time by cutting some things out that just aren't that important. If music is super important to you what you need to do is leverage something called the 80/20 rule. The 80/20 rule can help you not only get all the important and urgent stuff done faster but get all the important and non urgent things like your music making done in less time and with more quality. As a creative you need to learn this rule because it will help you get those things done that you want to get done and that means getting music made.

Stop Waiting

Stop waiting for inspiration to strike. It would be great if that were the case, if I'm sitting and eating a sandwich and all of a sudden I had this beautiful idea for a hit song. Most music is made by hard work. Most of the hit songs are written by songwriters that go to work every day and they write. They write hundreds and hundreds of songs, they record demos, they produce a lot of tracks and many never see the light of day. But that's how they get to the good stuff. You need to change your mindset and shift away from the wait for inspiration to strike mindset to create inspiration. But how do you force yourself to work on music making? By creating deadlines, deadlines that other people know about and hold you accountable to. Grab your calendar and decide what is it you want to do. Do you want to release an album? Do you want to release an EP? Do you want to mix for some new bands? Or do you just want to do a single? Whatever it is, decide a future. date on your calendar for when you're going to release it. Announce them publicly to at least one other person, ideally more than one person. You could go on social media and I say hey guys I'm going to release an EP on this date hold me accountable.

The moment you have a deadline things start to pick up and you feel that pressure. I've got to write some songs and get in studio. Even if you don't have time it creates time. Creating that forced deadline and then making it public will somehow magically help you find time even if it's pockets to get working. Somehow magically those pockets of time are more effective than they were if you had um limited open-ended time. This is because something called Parkinson's law, you can look it up it really does force you to get more done and get good work done.

Jump

Finally, get your music out there. You are no longer just a musician, producer, singer, songwriter or an artist, you are a brand. If you view yourself as just an artist then that means you're hoping that someone else will do everything for you. The things that used to be done for you by the industry which is to sign you and develop you as an artist get your stuff recorded, do all the marketing and promotion. This hasn't changed, if you want to grow and have people hear about you, you still have to market yourself. You still have to have do promotion, you still need to develop as an artist. All those things haven't gone away it's just that the burden has fallen on to you and you have to start thinking that you are the brand.

A brand is something that is sold, something that is marketed, something that people love and a brand is not a bad thing. Everybody is their own personal brand whether they believe it or not. If you want people to hear your music then you have to view what are all the duties that an entrepreneur or a business owner would do to get his or her product or service or brand out there. That will involve you doing a little bit of research and shifting your mindset from not being just a creative and a musician but to also being somewhat of a business owner. Incidentally that will involve learning about marketing, promotion, branding and all those things

Now related to you being a brand you got to view yourself as a content creator because we are in an age that loves to consume content. We love to scroll in our feeds and consume little bite-size content. It is a culture of boredom and a culture of getting lost in the black hole of more content. As an artist or musician you need to be a content creator. What that means for you is you don't just make music. Music is the hub of what you do but you don't just make albums and try to sell them or try to get them on the radio. You have to start viewing yourself as more than just I'm going to mix album or an EP or something. You are a content creator and your content happens to be music but it can also be other things. It could be video of you in your studio recording, it could be video of you songwriting, it could be an interview with you in the band, it could be live footage of you onstage at a show and so on. It could just be you talking to your fans about what you do on the weekends when you're not doing music or the inspiration for a song. There are a million things that you could do as an artist or band to create pieces of content short or long that would go alongside your other core content

The old rules involved just focusing on your music and the rest would come. Not today, you've got to be a brand and think about what it takes to be a brand and you have to be a content creator and create that engagement with your audience. Get your stuff out there, it doesn't have to be perfect. The old way was perfection, you had an artist or a band that was always presented perfectly. You'd be presented with your record which would sound amazing and be perfect and you'd be presented with a killer music video which would be perfect and amazing. That was the era that many of us grew up in.

Nowadays if you just want to release something once every two years and then nobody hears from you in between that time, well it just won't fly. Your audience will move on without you and they'll find someone else to to follow. You need to show up regularly. That could be every week, that could be every month, that could be every couple of months or it could be everyday if you've got the time. But how do you do that? You can't create polished amazing records or music videos that are full-blown productions every day or every week or even every month. Instead you need to embrace imperfection and start sharing stuff that's not finished. Don't spend forever on them just put it out there even if it's not perfect. Or don't release an album, instead just release singles once every month. Yeah you could spend ten more hours on it, but it might not be that much better and no one's gonna notice. Sorry to say, the moment you finish just it get it out there and then you can move onto the next project. Every time you move on to another project even if it's one song you will be approaching it with fresh ears, a fresh perspective and an increased awareness of what you can do better and what you did well last time.

Embrace the journey and enjoy it.

Thanks for Reading!

What did you think of, **Music Production Mastery: All You Need to Know About Producing Music, Songwriting, Music Theory and Creativity (Two Book Bundle)**

I know you could have picked any number of books to read, but you picked this book and for that I am extremely grateful.

I hope that it added at value and quality to your everyday life. If so, it would be really nice if you could share this book with your friends and family by posting to Facebook and Twitter.

If you enjoyed this book and found some benefit in reading this, I'd like to hear from you and hope that you could take some time to post a review. Your feedback and support will help this author to greatly improve his writing craft for future projects and make this book even better.

I want you, the reader, to know that your review is very important and so, if you'd like to leave a review, all you have to do is click here and away you go. I wish you all the best in your future success!

Also check out my other books:

In The Mix: Discover The Secrets to Becoming a Successful DJ

Music Production: Everything You Need To Know About Producing Music and Songwriting

Music Production: How to Produce Music, The Easy to Read Guide for Music Producers Introduction

Songwriting: Apply Proven Methods, Ideas and Exercises to Kickstart or Upgrade Your Songwriting

Thank you and good luck!

Tommy Swindali 2019

Claim This Now

In the Mix Discover the Secrets to Becoming a Successful DJ

If you have ever dreamed of being a DJ with people dancing to your music, all while having the time of your life, then this audiobook will show you how.

From the bedroom to the hottest clubs, to events and main-stage festivals. Whether you're a seasoned pro looking to enhance your current skills or a new, aspiring DJ looking to get started -

Whatever your level of experience, the wisdom in this audiobook is explosive, and it is an absolute must to skyrocketing your success as a DJ.

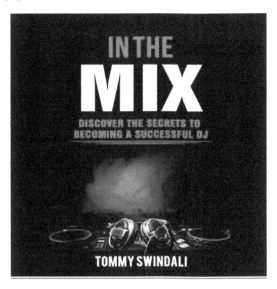

Discover "How to Find Your Sound"

http://musicprod.ontrapages.com/

Swindali music coaching/Skype lessons.

Email djswindali@gmail.com for info and pricing

CPSIA information can be obtained
at www.ICGtesting.com
Printed in the USA
BVHW032055171119
564094BV00001B/37/P

9 781913 397098